HOW TO COPE WITH YOUR PUPPY

How to Cope with Your Puppy

A guide to the behaviour and training of puppies and young dogs

Sarah Crockford

To all the puppies and young dogs I have had the pleasure to work with.

You have all taught me so much, and I have enjoyed our time together.

Copyright © 2022 Sarah Crockford

This is a general guide to the training and behaviour of puppies and young dogs. Chronic or serious issues may require the help of a professional trainer or behaviourist, especially for cases involving aggression. Always seek veterinary advice if your puppy's behaviour changes suddenly, as there may be an underlying health cause.

The questions and answers in part three are based on multiple cases seen by Sarah, and are not about specific owners or puppies.

The first edition of this book was published in 2020 (as 'How to Cope with your Puppy and Young Dog').

This second edition ('How to Cope with your Puppy') was published in 2022.

www.sarahcrockford.com

Contents

Introduction

This second edition of 'How to Cope with your Puppy' includes several new chapters, plus a 'Frequently Asked Questions' section. These questions cover most of the common issues I've been asked about over the years. Hopefully you will learn a lot from the answers given, and will be able to try out some of the suggestions.

Puppies do a lot of learning and growing up in a short space of time, and need lots of training and careful management to avoid issues developing. They turn into teenagers around five months of age, and become adult dogs around two years of age. Their many months as an adolescent can be especially challenging, leaving us wondering why we ever decided to get a puppy in the first place. But above all, it's an exciting, fun-filled, and incredibly rewarding experience.

I hope you enjoy reading this guide. If you get to the end and still can't find an answer to your particular issues, you can contact me for more information – you can find details on my website:

www.sarahcrockford.com

Happy training!

Sarah Crockford

Part 1: Growing up

Time with mum

You might not have a lot of control over what happens to your puppy before you collect them, but you *can* be careful with your choice of breeder. It's important to visit the litter and choose your puppy, so you can assess their behaviour, and the behaviour of their mum. Ask yourself lots of questions during the visit: you should feel comfortable in the environment where the puppies have been born, and are now living. You need to be happy with their mum's health and temperament (and be sure it *is* their mum and not a substitute, which can happen with puppy-farmed dogs). When you interact with the puppies, make sure they have healthy skin, coat and eyes, and appear alert. Then think about which one would be the most suitable one for your home and family. You might want to avoid the one that's cowering at the back, or the one that leaps all over you and won't settle. Although their behaviour is not set in stone at this stage, it's an important clue for their general development - ask yourself how these behaviours could affect things once they're older and a lot bigger.

You can also observe your potential puppy's interaction with their brothers and sisters. They should play well, taking it in turns to chase or wrestle, without being a bully or being continuously picked on. Their mum should be attentive, and should direct and correct their behaviour when necessary; but not be overly controlling or defensive.

Puppies are born helpless, and rely completely on their mum for food, warmth and protection. Their eyes open around two weeks of age, although it's several more weeks before they see things 'normally'. Their ears open at a similar time, and again development continues for a few more weeks. Solid puppy food is usually introduced by the breeder around four weeks of age, to complement the milk still being provided by their mum.

Mum will need to stimulate them to wee and poo until they're around three to four weeks of age, then they'll become a little more independent and move away from their bed to eliminate.

This means that by four weeks of age, puppies are able to learn about their environment, interact with it, and become curious about exploring. They continue to gain confidence over the following few weeks, until they leave for their new home. What happens during this time will affect their behaviour later in life, which is why choosing the right breeder is so important.

If they leave mum too early (six weeks and younger), they will lose out on valuable lessons, including bite inhibition. This is when they discover they can hurt others with their teeth, and learn to reduce the force of their jaws while playing. Although it's a lesson that has to be continued when they get to their new home, it's started early by their mum and littermates. Also, having the security of the 'nest' to go back to, enables puppies to develop the confidence to explore while still having guidance from mum when they start doing anything unsafe. If they lose this too soon, they can become anxious, or alternatively could become overly-confident and very independent (making later training much harder).

But if they leave their mum and littermates too late (nine weeks and over), their new owner will be missing out on valuable time to teach their puppy new routines, and creating the strong bond with them that will enable easier training. The older a puppy is, the harder this work can be, especially if they haven't been taught these things by the breeder. They may become frightened

3

by 'everyday' household sounds and activities, not know how to deal with meeting strangers, and not know how to cope alone. If a puppy is fully vaccinated but never been on a walk, they could become very scared about the experience.

Moving home

Most puppies will leave their mother and littermates around 7-8 weeks of age, and won't be fully vaccinated and allowed out until 11-13 weeks of age or possibly later (depending on the vaccination schedule offered by your vets). This short time-frame should be focused on settling them into a routine (including toilet training); and getting them used to all the sights, sounds, smells, and textures in the house and garden. You will also need to begin obedience training, especially recall. Even very young puppies are capable of learning a surprising amount.

Vaccinations

Vaccination ages can vary, and vets usually recommend waiting a week after the last jab before you can allow your puppy out and about. But your puppy may be restricted to your house and garden only until they are about thirteen weeks old. Although there are risks associated with them being in the garden (for example foxes wandering through), or when people enter the house (and inadvertently bring in bacteria or viruses on their shoes), as long as these risks are minimised, the benefits usually far outweigh any concerns.

A puppy who is toilet trained by taking them in the garden regularly learns the process faster, and is much easier to live with. In addition, playtime in the garden is joyful, as well as being a useful way of getting rid of their excess energy. Any specific health concerns you have should be discussed with your vet.

Early lessons

Between getting your puppy around seven or eight weeks of age, and when they're allowed out around eleven or thirteen weeks of age, there are a lot of lessons that need to be covered. Your puppy needs to be toilet trained, have learnt to respond to their name, and preferably know 'Sit' and 'Down', and can be directed to go in their crate or bed where they will happily settle. They also need to get used to short car journeys (not just to the vets!), and be carried around town centres etc. so they get used to seeing/ hearing/ smelling all the things they will experience after they're allowed out. They also need to be used to their collar and lead, and know how to walk nicely (in the house and garden) without pulling, playing with the lead, or getting scared.

Handling

Handling is important to ensure a puppy is used to being picked up, accepts wearing a collar or harness, and can tolerate being groomed, having claws trimmed, and their bottom/ teeth/ eyes/ ears checked and cleaned. You can also get them used to what vets, groomers, and dog show judges will do. A puppy needs to remain calm, and learn to tolerate (or even to welcome) what's happening. This needs lots of teaching, as puppies will quickly learn to resist being handled, and can get quite resistant and bitey.

The key is to reward them *a lot*. Keep sessions short to begin with, and gradually build up their ability to stay still for longer. Make sure they're okay about other people doing this too: your vet or groomer will thank you for this.

The early fear period

Puppies sometimes have a 'fear period' at around ten weeks of age, when they suddenly appear scared of things they were okay with before. This can last a few days, and isn't the time to do new things, or take them out for their first walk or trip to town. It can significantly affect your progress with habituation (getting them used to objects and sounds) and socialisation (getting them used to people, dogs, and other animals). If the worst happens, and they get scared of something, you will need to add de-sensitisation to your training as well. This can be a slow process, as you need to reward them for coping while the trigger is small enough (e.g. a car a long way away), gradually building them up to the level it was when it frightened them.

One moment at a time...

Puppies live in the present - reacting to stimuli around them, and learning what links with what. Any training and management you do with them also needs to be done *in the moment* it happens. If they're trying to climb in the dishwasher, you need to deal with that straight away, so they learn it's a bad thing to do. If they wee in the right place in the garden, they need a suitable reward delivered just after they've finished going. If they're frightened by a loud noise, help them to realise they're ok, and you're ok, and that they can be calm when it happens again. Support them through fear without encouraging it; and reward calmness, curiosity and bravery. Try not to over-face them. By giving them a fighting chance of coping, you'll encourage the development of confidence rather than anxiety. React to what's happening with your puppy, and try to get used to predicting what is *about* to happen, so you're ready to provide guidance at the right moment.

Heading into the outside world

Once your puppy is fully vaccinated, the real work begins. They're in puppyhood, and relatively compliant, until they start becoming a teenager around 20 weeks of age (five months). That's a short window of opportunity.

Their first walk

Once they're allowed out you need to focus on their lead training; recall when off-lead; and getting them used to a huge number and variety of things. Habituation is getting them used to objects and sounds; socialisation is getting them used to people, dogs, and other animals. It's important to go at your puppy's pace, and not to over-face them. Most puppies will bounce back from a scary experience as long as you stay calm, and jolly them along (and provided they didn't get physically hurt). However, sometimes one bad experience is all it takes to convince them that, for example, *all* dogs are scary. You will then need to do lots of re-training to make sure this doesn't become a permanent habit. Some dogs, especially German Shepherds, will experience a second fear period when they're around 10 months old. This is not the time to do new or potentially scary things.

Tantrums

All puppies and adolescent dogs have the odd tantrum, but they can occur more often in certain individuals. Tantrums happen when a puppy feels they're not getting the desired outcome from something, and when they have a build-up of emotions and energy. They are usually worse when a puppy is overtired and/ or overstimulated. If you're able to stay calm under pressure, it's a good idea to stay in the moment with your puppy, and wait for the tantrum to pass. Then you can praise them, and continue with the training. If you're holding on to them, and they resist by squirming and biting, try to maintain your hold on their collar/ harness/ body with quiet persistence until they take a breath and relax. Then let them go: this may need repeating several times. You don't need to say anything during the tantrum. In fact, it's best to keep quiet, and just focus on their behaviour and yours. They need to learn that tantrums don't get them what they want: you need to be ready to reward them when they give up, and look to you for an alternative. But if you get easily frustrated or frightened by a grumpy puppy, it's best to exit the room or steer them towards their pen or rest area, and leave them to calm down by themselves.

It's natural for puppies and young dogs to test boundaries, and they will go through several phases of this while they're growing up. Just keep teaching them the same things, and make sure everyone else does as well – consistency is the key to success. If the tantrums become serious, and you feel it's heading towards aggression, then it's best to chat to your vet, who may be able to recommend a behaviourist or trainer. It's much better to sort out problems early, rather than ignore them in the hope they'll 'grow out of it'.

Teenage angst

When puppies reach five months of age, they begin to practise adult behaviours, and become more independent. This will continue in waves until they settle down as an adult. Depending on breed, this can be 18 months, or over two years of age: some seem to remain teenagers for life.

Hormones

Hormone levels are higher by six months of age, and this is usually the earliest that dogs are neutered. They will probably think a bit more competitively, and they will notice if you give in too easily, and may learn to ignore your requests. For instance, you might have had a puppy who always came back when called, only for them to start running off and appearing deaf to your calls.

Their behaviour at this age isn't all down to hormones, but it adds an extra layer to the reason your puppy has suddenly become distracted, and no longer sees you as the most important thing in the world.

Demanding behaviour

As a puppy grows up and experiences life, they form their own mind about things, and know what they want. They also learn what gets our attention, and that will usually be something we don't want them to do. They learn how much to push us before we give in to their requests, which is why patience and consistency are so important.

Let's say your puppy has started barking, and you're beginning to find it really annoying. You'll first need to work out *why* they're barking, as this affects the way you deal with it. Barking is *communication*: your puppy is trying to tell you (or someone else, or an animal or object) something. Once you know why, try to find a way to prevent the barking. For example, if your dog is bored, give them more to do so they won't get bored and bark. Or if they're scared of being left on their own, train them to accept the situation without getting worried. If they're barking at the birds in the garden, work on 'leave', and distract them with play. If they're nervous of visitors to the house or dogs they see on walks, do some de-sensitisation training with them. If they're demanding food or attention, make sure you time the rewards to arrive when they're quiet. So, throw the ball when they *stop* barking, feed them *only when* they are able to sit quietly for twenty seconds, stroke them *only when* they're calm etc. Once you've begun to reward what you *do* want (staying calm and not barking), then you can interrupt the barking when it does happen (e.g. saying 'Enough!' assertively). But be quick to redirect their behaviour, or they will simply go back to what they were doing before.

Keep calm, and carry on training

It's important for you to be able to stay calm and consistent, and go back a few steps in training if you need to. For example, if they've been running off on walks, you could keep them on lead for a week of re-training before trying again. Provided you have done all the foundation work, and you keep doing the same training (even during the difficult days), the 'teenage stage' should just be a phase. Teenage dog brains, like humans, undergo a lot of rewiring, learning and adapting. It's not easy for them to concentrate, or to accept being told what to do!

Training needs to continue throughout their teenage months, as you need to instil patterns of good behaviour. In other words, you need to form the habits you want them to have as adults, even though it's tempting to ignore what's happening in the hope they'll 'settle down' as they get older. They might, but then again they might not, so it's generally best not to take the risk. Unwanted behaviour patterns learnt during this time are likely to remain permanent. Your perfect puppy will only become a perfect adult if you put the work in!

Although behaviour will alter (for the better or worse) as they grow up, any sudden and unexplained changes in behaviour or health (e.g. aggression, toileting more often, scratching their skin etc) need to be discussed with your vet.

Part 2: Management and basic training

Toileting

When we get a puppy, apart from enjoying their company, the main focus of our lives suddenly becomes the frequency of urination, the consistency of faeces, and *where* these deposits are made. Toileting can be a real headache to get right, and can cause a lot of friction within a family (including who's turn it is to supervise, and who's using the 'right' method).

Location, location, location

You need to be clear in your intentions about *where* you want the weeing and pooing to happen. If you have a garden, it's a good idea to get your puppy used to going out every time they need to eliminate. If you have a chosen a specific area of the garden for them to head for, this requires extra work, as you'll have to keep them on a lead (and stay with them) until they've performed in the chosen location. Most owners are just thankful their puppy isn't doing it in the house, and therefore don't really care *where* they do it in the garden.

Within the house, you can put puppy pads or newspaper on the floor. These might be within a crate or pen, by the door leading to the garden (for times where you're not around to let them out), or anywhere they tend to go without you seeing (behind the sofa, by the door to the living room, under the table etc.). Although you might not like the idea of them toileting in the house, if they can be trained to use pads or paper, at least the clean-up becomes easier, and it will be quicker to train them to go in the garden only. If they are weeing and pooing everywhere (carpets, wood floors, under the sofa, on the mat by the front door etc.) training becomes a much longer, and more involved, process. If you live in a flat, you might consider having a litter tray (like you would for a cat or house rabbit) with a puppy pad in it. This can become a permanent place for them to wee/poo, as you might not be able to get them out as frequently. If you have a covered, and safe, balcony, you could have a litter tray out there; otherwise choose an appropriate location within the flat.

Pads within a crate or pen are particularly useful at night so their bedding stays clean, and your puppy isn't fretting about needing to go out. If you don't include pads, and hear them wake up in the night and cry, you will need to get up and take them into the garden, or risk them learning to soil their bedding.

Reward them for getting it right

Escort your puppy outside (whatever the weather conditions) every thirty minutes or so until they show signs of being clean for longer. If you know they need to go, take them out every ten minutes until they do go: don't leave them unsupervised in the house until then.

Reward *every* wee and poo outside (or on pads if toilet training indoors) in the beginning, with a tasty food treat. Then gradually reward less often e.g. save it for the times when you know your puppy has 'held on', or when they go on cue. Keep rewarding with food until there have been no accidents in the house for at least two weeks. But it's a good idea to continue verbally praising them when they go in the right place, and do this well into their teenage months.

You can add a cue to toileting e.g. 'Busy Busy!' or 'Go wee wee!': but try to choose something you will not say in any other situation. Always reward them when they perform on cue, even if it's just verbal praise. If you want your puppy to learn to 'ask' to go out, you must be around to spot when they *do* ask. They might simply walk towards or sit by the door, give a little whine, or look at you etc. Alternatively, you can hang bells from the door handle, and teach your puppy to nudge them with their nose. Some dogs never learn the habit to actively ask to go out, so it's important to take them out regularly.

Prevent them from getting it wrong

If you choose to use pads, make sure you have a large crate, or a pen attached to a small crate. If they are loose in a room, put the pads by the door that leads to the outside, and anywhere else you notice your puppy has accidents. It's important to restrict their access to areas you *don't* want accidents in. Puppies often prefer to wee on something absorbent e.g. grass rather than concrete. If they only have a choice between patio and carpet, they're likely to wait until they get inside. Clean up any accidents in the house thoroughly (with a product that gets rid of the enzymes in the urine e.g. a spray bought from a pet shop, or a biological washing solution), otherwise they will simply go back to where they went before. Supervision is really important. If you see them preparing to wee/poo in the house (sniffing, looking distracted, moving towards a door, circling, crouching etc), interrupt them, and get them outside or on a pad.

If your puppy sleeps in your bedroom, you will be more aware if they stir in the early hours and need to wee or poo. With very young puppies, you can have some pads set up in the bathroom to save you having to go outside. After the toilet trip it's straight back to bed: keep it all very low-key. Most older puppies who've had some toilet training will hold on during the night, unless they didn't eliminate before bed; or drank too much before going to sleep; or if they have a health issue.

Punishing accidents can make things worse

Although you might be tempted to, never tell a puppy off for toilet training errors. It could cause them to hide next time, or make them generally more nervous (so they're more likely to have accidents), and it will sour the relationship between you and your puppy. It is your responsibility to toilet train your puppy: don't blame them when you get it wrong. If you miss the signs that they wanted to wee/ poo and they've already started, it's too late, just quietly clear up the mess. Promise yourself you will catch the moment next time. Interruption is okay, as long as it's effective, and you can get them out to the correct place quick enough. Otherwise, all you get is a trail of wee or poo which will take longer to clean up, and you will have an unhappy puppy who won't want to toilet in front of you next time.

Sometimes young dogs will start marking indoors (males will begin to cock their leg when they become teenagers). This is the only circumstance when you would use verbal telling off to stop weeing in the house. But your timing has to be spot on: you have to catch the *intention* to mark – afterwards is too late. Clean up any urine marks thoroughly. Walk your puppy more often, so they do all their marking outside. Castration may lessen marking behaviour: you can discuss this with your vet. However, marking in the house is often due to insecurity, and is never done out of 'spite'. It's important to work out what's upsetting them – change that, and they won't need to mark or have accidents, and you won't be tempted to tell them off.

Phases

Sometimes puppies go through phases. The toilet training will be going brilliantly, and then they'll suddenly seem to forget how to ask to go out, or they stop being clean through the night, or they start weeing in a room they've never had an accident in before. This might be linked to anxiety, with something upsetting them and causing them to need to toilet quickly. It might just last a day or so, for no apparent reason, and then they go back to normal and are clean again. Sometimes it requires a change in routine. This might involve feeding them at an earlier time, or making their last wee in the garden later; or you might have to set your alarm a bit earlier so you can get them out before they resort to going in the house; or you can take away their water last thing in the evening so they don't 'top up' during the night. Experiment with small changes (don't change too much at once or that will cause more anxiety), and see what works.

If you think you have a serious behavioural issue developing, or a health issue (e.g. weeing more frequently than normal, or the consistency of their poo changing), then it's important you have a chat with your vet. They may recommend a change in diet, medication (if they suspect a urine infection or a bacterial infection in the gut), or they may point you in the direction of a behaviourist or trainer.

Recall

We all want to be able to call out our puppy's name, and for them to come running to us, *every* time we ask. But our puppies, and especially adolescent dogs, need a good reason to come back. Some fuss and attention might be enough for young puppies, but older ones will need more motivation. A toy might do it, but the most common incentive is food – tasty treats, not just the boring kibble they get at mealtimes. If these rewards aren't available (and sometimes even when they are), young dogs prefer to carry on doing what they were doing: exploring, sticking their nose into rabbit tunnels, running through muddy puddles, following joggers, chasing squirrels etc. They need a *very* good reason to stop all that and come back to us. As well as food, toys and praise, being released to play or run is also a reward. So, when they do a good recall, once you've given them a treat, let them go again – it's a good way to prove you're not trying to end their fun. Make sure when you *do* ask for them to come to you, they wait close enough that you could take hold of their collar. You can even make this part of the process: call your dog, they run back, you hold their collar, and *then* give them their food treat.

Practice recall lots during a walk, and mix up on-lead and off-lead walking. If your puppy realises you only call them at the end of the walk, when they go back on lead, they are going to be more resistant to listening to your instructions.

Cues and commands

A command is a strongly spoken instruction, one which you expect to be followed, and has an air of punishment about it. As such, it can be useful for stopping behaviours ('bad dog', 'stop it', 'leave it', 'stay there' etc). Commands are not so good for inviting puppies to come towards us (if you shout 'come here!' in a cross voice, your dog is likely to stay away). Recall requires our dogs to *choose* to come to us, even if they don't want to, and the last thing we need is to add anxiety to the situation, and make them worry about returning. So, recall is really a *cue*.

A cue is an action, word or noise that, when linked to a reward, strengthens the behaviour being trained. An excited 'Buddy, come here!' with a piece of cheese being held out, will create the behaviour of returning when called. If done well, the cue can be decreased in strength, but the behaviour will remain as strong – as long as the reward is sufficient for your puppy to continue complying. It's important not to get rid of food rewards too soon – it takes many weeks for a habit to be formed, and even then, teenage dogs will need a lot of convincing! Calling in an excited way comes easily to children - not so much for adults. But it's important you try as many things to encourage your puppy to come to you as possible. You might need to keep saying their name in a high-pitched voice, or clap your hands (as if applauding), or crouch down and pat the ground, or pretend to run in the opposite direction, or make lots of silly noises to get their attention. Body posture is as important as what you say, and how you say it. If you're standing upright and rigid, and 'commanding', your puppy won't be as keen. Soften your frame, and invite them towards you. Be happy at their approach.

Choose your cues and stick to them. It could be your voice 'Bobby, Come!', or a whistle (e.g. 3 blasts – try to make it different from other calls you hear in your usual walking areas); deaf dogs can be trained using a vibrating collar. Remember that *a cue is only as strong as their desire to come back*. A whistle is not a magic device that makes puppies return: they come back if they *choose* to come back. You have to find ways to develop their willingness and motivation.

Determination

Be careful when you ask for a recall, because once you've asked, you have to see it through. Your dog needs to learn that it's easier to listen and respond the first time, so they can get back to whatever it was they were doing without being nagged further. Remember to call them back lots, not just when they spot dogs or squirrels, or at the end of the walk. A lot of dogs learn that a recall cue means 'look around to see if there's a new dog to play with' or 'stay away because my lead's going back on'. Vary walks so sometimes they're on a short lead, sometimes on an extendable one, and sometimes off lead. Practise recall in all these circumstances, help them to learn to respond whenever you ask for their attention.

You can do partial recalls as well, when you change direction on a walk. Call out 'this way!', then go down a different path – your puppy should catch up to you, run past you and explore ahead. They don't need a food reward for this, because running off in a new direction *is* the reward.

Be assertive when asking, but don't sound cross. Save that for when they're doing something really bad like eating a rabbit carcass, or rolling in fox poo, or choosing to ignore you by looking away. Use general verbal corrections such as 'leave', 'stop it' or 'enough'. You might also have a version of their name you shout out when you're trying to get their attention (like mums do with their children), e.g. '*Alfred*!' shouted in a manner that means 'you'd better start listening to me', which will be in contrast to a light-hearted 'Alfie, come here, good boy!' when they're doing the right thing. If the verbal command doesn't work, you will have to get closer, the faster the better (to stop the fun they're having), so be prepared to run towards them. Then try to get their attention again. If they're still not listening to you, get between them and the thing they're focused on. Once they're able to concentrate on you, switch to verbal praise, put them on lead, and do some training. If they're trying to eat something they shouldn't, use the 'leave' cue every time they look at it, and reward them with food for walking away from it, or looking at you instead. Always reward when they listen to you and come back (even if you had to hold their collar to move them away from what they were doing). Smile and tell them they're good, but save the best rewards for when they listened the first time you called them.

Prevention

If your puppy is likely to run off and explore, get themselves in trouble, pester people for attention, run up to every dog they see, chase cats, rabbits and foxes etc. and not listen to your requests – then don't let them off lead! Why set yourself and your puppy up to fail? Do some more training, and try again another day. Or use a long training line (depending on the breed and size of your puppy) so you can enforce a recall (i.e. short pulls on the lead until they comply). If you feel they haven't had enough exercise, then get creative – jog with them on a lead for a short time; play more in the garden; and find new areas to walk in. Although you can't control the distractions that will occur, through training you can control your dog's *responses* to those distractions.

Early Obedience Training

By starting your training as soon as you get your puppy means you have head start moulding the dog you wish to live with. Puppies are very willing and able to learn new things, as long as the instructions are clear, and they are given a reason for complying with the requests.

Rewards

Using verbal praise (like 'good boy', 'oh you're so clever', 'such a good girl', 'well done!'), is a great way to enforce your puppy's good behaviour, and it improves your bond with them. Puppies love to be told how wonderful they are, and your tone of voice (happy, excited and loving) is even more important than the words you use. But verbal praise won't always be as effective as foods rewards, especially when there's something as exciting to do as chase a pigeon, jump up at a visitor, or eat cake that's been left on the table.

Physical fussing is enjoyed by most puppies and young dogs, but during training most prefer working for toys or food rewards. In fact, a lot of puppies will actively step away from being stroked during training, or even flash their teeth in annoyance. Over-fussing can become a form of punishment (making training much harder), or over-excite or annoy them so much that it makes their behaviour less controllable (they might start biting more, or listening to you less). So, although handling and grooming are important lessons, they can be trained using food rewards; and although cuddle time is important, it can be done during restful moments, rather than while your puppy is wide awake and wanting action.

The use of toys in play and training should be encouraged as it uses up their energy, makes them work with you, and will help keep them focused in the park (instead of running off after other dogs or wildlife). There are balls they can chase, find and fetch; and tuggy toys to pull and shake. Other toys, like Kongs, can have food inside for independent play.

Timing

Remember to be careful what you're rewarding. If you're about to throw a ball and your puppy is barking excitedly, it's best to wait until they're quiet and still before throwing the ball – otherwise you will be encouraging them to bark. Likewise, if you're wanting to play tug but your puppy keeps trying to rip it out your hand or is biting you instead, you need to develop some rules for 'appropriate play'. Invite them to start tugging with a cue 'tug-tug!', and ask them to stop if things are getting crazy (e.g. 'drop'). Then make them sit calmly to wait for the next round. Reward the right behaviours.

Using food treats is the best reinforcer to use with the majority of dogs. It can be as a lure to teach them how to sit, lie down, go to bed, and roll over (using the food like a magnet – wherever their nose goes, the rest of them will follow); and as a reward for performing a behaviour like stay, leave, recall and walking to heel. When you first start training your puppy, you will need to reward them lots. Then gradually start to only reward the best attempts. Don't wean them off the rewards too quickly though: there are many new lessons that need to be learnt, maintained and improved before they become reliable.

Loose lead walking

The more you do now, the easier it becomes. Even if your puppy isn't fully vaccinated, you can still train them to walk by your side in the house and garden. The thing to keep in mind is that walking out the house is (generally) an exciting experience for a puppy or young dog. They want to get somewhere, find friends, indulge in interesting smells, be let off the lead to play… and they want to get to all of these things *as quickly as possible*. To walk slowly and calmly is a hard lesson for them to learn, and requires a lot of patience from us in order to teach it. It's also a lesson that has to be continuously repeated, on every walk, every day.

Young dogs will test us, to make sure the rules are the same (they'd love to break them and be able to race off), so they will test our reserve on *every walk*. Yes it's annoying, but it's a natural part of growing up for them, and it's a commitment we as owners have to make if we want to develop a well-behaved adult dog that is a pleasure to walk.

Teaching 'heel'

To teach your puppy to walk to heel (where their shoulder or ribcage is roughly in line with your legs as you walk) reward them with treats for being in the right position. Use a word such as 'heel' or 'close' while they're getting it right, so they develop a link between that word and walking nicely. If they move out of position, encourage them back to the right place, and start again. You need to gradually lengthen the time between treats, until you're relying mainly on verbal praise. This is great for walking past distractions such as people, dogs, cats and livestock, and it means your puppy is under *close control*.

Relaxed walking

Most walks can be a little less formal, and you can allow your puppy to wander ahead or to the side. They can be on a longer lead, or even an extendable one. But the main rule is that they must remain clam, and they mustn't pull. You want to encourage your puppy to remain attentive if you talk to them or call them back. If they start pulling, act quickly to remind them how to walk at the speed you have chosen. This is *relaxed walking*. There's no specific cue needed for this. You can use verbal praise to tell them they're doing the right thing. By allowing them to explore and sniff you are using environmental rewards, which means you won't need to use food rewards (these are reserved for 'formal heel' position and for recall). If they start to pull on the lead, or get over-excited and start dashing around, the rewards must stop (i.e. stop praising them, don't allow them to walk on, don't allow them to sniff the thing they want to get to, and don't allow them to meet the dog they've seen). Once they're calmer, start walking again.

Stop-start

If the pulling is stronger, or your dog's focus is not on you, the first thing you need to do is stand still. Only move forward when your dog makes an effort to tune into you e.g. steps backwards, turns to face you, moves a front leg towards you, walks to your side/ behind you, or looks at you for longer than two seconds. As soon as they've acted, you need to walk on, but be ready to stand still again if they pull. This sequence has to happen *every* time they pull. As long as you get your timing right, and you are consistent (i.e. you do it all the time however annoying it is), your dog will realise that pulling is useless, as it doesn't get them to where they want to go. They will gradually pull less, and even when they do, it will take them less time to re-focus.

Turn around

If they still can't refocus, turn around and walk in the opposite direction until your puppy agrees to go that way. Then turn back to your original route. An alternative version is to make your dog walk around your body - they will end up facing the same way, but stop them before they walk too far ahead again. Keep repeating this manoeuvre until they can stand quietly by your side. These techniques turn pulling into a 'bigger deal'. As long as you're consistent, your puppy will learn it's not worth pulling if they end up having to walk away, or walk circles round you. If you think you would have to stand still for a long time, or turning away doesn't work, it's best to simply change direction, and walk somewhere else. Try again another day when they're more receptive.

Let the lead do the talking

Once you start walking, there will be a point when they begin to pull. Try not to keep a constant pressure on the lead, or your puppy will simply lean on this pressure. Make lots of very small movements of the lead back and forward with your hand (a gentle reminder rather than a pull). It means there's nothing to lean on, and it acts as communication to your dog – a warning that you are still connected, and you will act if they try to pull more. If your dog responds to this, you can keep walking. If they don't, stand still, stop-start, or turn-around.

Collars, harnesses and head-halters

Most of your walking training will be done with your puppy on a collar and lead. But if you want to walk your puppy without having to take time to train them (e.g. if you're out with young children and need to keep moving), you will find a harness useful. They won't teach your puppy not to pull, but they won't undo the training you've been doing with the collar.

Some young dogs develop a habit of backing out of their collar to run away, or go and do their own thing. If they have a few successes, they will get better at it. Other than a bit of retraining, you can use a 'half-check' collar. These are generally made of strong fabric, with a connecting piece of metal chain. The collar tightens enough when pulled that it won't slip over a dog's head, but it won't continue to tighten (unlike a full-check or slip-lead); meaning it's less damaging to their neck and windpipe, whilst also ensuring they stay safe.

If your dog is over six months of age and is really strong, or has learnt to pull you off-balance (or pull the lead out your hand), you might want to consider a head halter (e.g. Halti, Gentle Leader or Dogmatic) whilst you're doing some re-training. You will need lots of treats and praise to help your dog get used to this, as most dogs will naturally find it unsettling.

There are also different types of body harness available that encourage good walking behaviour, often with two points of contact (to be used with a double ended lead), which will give you much more control over their movements.

Fear and anger on walks

Most lead walking issues will stem from excitement, and a determination to get somewhere quickly. But sometimes a puppy might become afraid and want to run home. They're unlikely to respond to food, or verbal cues to walk to heel and refocus. Work out what they're afraid of, and help them through it. Next time, use treats to de-sensitise them to that trigger. Don't let them drag you home, or you will be reinforcing their fear. Wait with them until they're calmer. Smaller puppies can be picked up, but don't overdo the fussing or they will continue to need this whenever they become fearful.

Some puppies can become defensive when on a lead, particularly if they've had a bad encounter with another dog. They might start acting aggressively towards other dogs, and this can quickly get worse if not addressed. Reward good responses with praise and food treats. Try to prevent it happening by anticipating the problem, and not getting too close to other dogs. You can correct growling/ barking/ lunging behaviour verbally (e.g. 'enough!') and with a couple of pulls on the lead, but remember that it's best to focus on rewarding them for getting things right. If they don't immediately respond, walk them away from the issue, and try again when you're a bit further away. It will take lots of de-sensitisation for a puppy to become less stressed on walks.

Jumping up at people

Puppies really love to jump up at people – it might be you and your family, visitors to the house, or people they meet on walks (both on lead and off lead). Mostly it's because of excitement, but sometimes it can be a symptom of an adolescent dog trying to control the behaviour of others.

Big rewards

Most dogs, especially puppies, jump up at people because it's fun and it works. It usually gets someone's attention, and often results in them being stroked or talked to (even if that person is actually pushing them away or telling them off). If you ignore your puppy, or simply walk away the instant they jump up, they will begin to realise it's a rubbish way of getting your attention. You must make sure that all visitors, and anyone else who meets your puppy, only talks to them/ strokes them/ plays with them if your puppy keeps *all four paws on the ground*. If people won't comply with this, you will either have to prevent their access to your puppy, or hold your puppy's collar (or stand on their lead), so they can't physically jump. Don't allow other people to spoil your plans for a well-behaved dog.

You can't rely on just ignoring the jumping up, without doing any other training, as puppies and young dogs who are persistent will find other ways to get attention. This could be barking, grabbing clothes, or even biting your ankles. Always aim to teach them the behaviour you want to see, which is probably *sitting calmly* in front of you. Other behaviours you can encourage include: standing still, lying down and asking for a belly rub, getting a toy, running after a ball, or doing a trick for a treat. Make sure you also do this when visitors come, and when you meet people in the park etc., and try to get them involved in the training.

Attention and focus

Train a strong recall, so that if your puppy is about to jump up at someone, you can call them away (and reward them) before they get it wrong. Alternatively, you can remind them to sit or wait. Keep your cool: there's little point in telling off a dog who's already jumped up, because by then it's too late. If you want to use verbal punishment, it must be done at the precise moment your dog is about to jump. Say a sharp 'No!', then change to a happy tone if they get it right ('Good boy for not jumping!'), then quickly refocus them onto something else. If you give them the opportunity, they will simply go back to what they were going to do i.e. jumping up.

Use your body language to make it clear what you expect. If necessary, stand between your dog and the person they want to jump up at. Defend the person, only letting your dog approach them if they're calm. You will need to reward the person for being calm too! The last thing you need is for them to be excited about meeting your dog, as they will encourage the jumping behaviour. Once you have your puppy under control put them on lead, and walk away if necessary. But ideally, you need to hang around long enough for the lesson to be completed – your dog standing or sitting quietly while the person strokes them. If this happens, give your dog lots of verbal praise, with a food treat afterwards, to make it even more meaningful.

If your puppy often jumps up because they're over-excited or full of energy, play with them for a bit first, or take them on a walk away from other people. Once your puppy is in a more receptive mindset, they'll be ready for their lessons!

Chewing and Biting

The reasons why puppies chew and bite include: play; being over-tired or over-excited, and losing self-control; stress/ fear/ anxiety/ frustration/ anger; controlling movement or resources; teething; trying to escape being handled or moved; boredom; attention seeking; dietary needs; and lack of early lessons. That's a long list of possibilities. So, it's important to try and work out what's going on, before you try to make changes to improve things.

The reasons puppies chew

Puppies investigate their world through tasting and chewing things. If you leave them unsupervised, or without enough things of their own to chew and play with, they will experiment on furniture, carpets, plants, books, shoes, children's toys, food packets, wallets, remote controls etc. If they do make a mistake, interrupt them, and immediately redirect them to something they *are allowed* to chew. Then prevent them making the same mistake again. Don't be tempted to chase them if they've taken something e.g. a shoe, or you'll turn it into a game, and actually reward the behaviour. Stay calm, and approach with a treat. Use it as an opportunity to teach a 'drop' or 'give', where your puppy will calmly let you take something out their mouth for a food reward. Then prevent it happening again, for example by making sure all shoes remain behind a baby gate, so your puppy can't get to them.

Chewing also happens due to dietary issues, teething, to relieve anxiety, or if they're angry about something (which can be the result of them being over-tired). Having more toys available, or giving them Kongs stuffed with wet puppy food, often help solve these problems. All puppies go through phases of chewing linked to teething, and they start getting their adult teeth around 18 weeks of age. Cool or frozen items can help sooth discomfort in their mouth, and there are also specific teething toys available from pet shops.

If your puppy is scratching and chewing doorways, they might be suffering with separation anxiety, which means they've developed a desperate need to escape and find you. Use obedience training to help them learn to stay without always having company, and provide a really good edible chew toy to tempt them – a Kong filled with puppy food is one example.

The reasons puppies bite

If you or others are being bitten because your puppy is over-tired or over-stimulated, then you need to put them somewhere they can calm down, with something suitable to chew. If they are frustrated (but not ready for a sleep), you need to continue training or playing, but make things easier for them to understand and achieve. Biting is communication. You just need to work out what's going on *before* your puppy resorts to biting (mainly because it hurts, but also, it's not a behaviour we want them to practise). Puppies bite because of stress, fear, anger, or just because they've learnt it works. If their life and management is a little calmer, and all their physical and emotional needs are met, then the amount of unwanted biting and chewing should reduce.

Biting, and chewing the wrong things can be improved with training. Remember to encourage good behaviour by providing alternatives, and giving them lots of praise and attention when they're getting it right, as well as preventing them from getting it wrong next time.

Containment

Barriers (crates, pens, baby gates and doors) can prevent puppies from making mistakes when they can't be supervised, or when their behaviour is negatively affecting other people, animals, or their own learning. Dogs of any age should always have toys and things of their own to play with and chew, and somewhere comfortable to rest and sleep.

If they find being left in a crate/ pen/ room difficult, the use of special treats (like a Kong stuffed with wet puppy food) will help them associate these areas as good places to be. Crates (if big enough) can be used for as long as they are necessary. For example, if you're using one to help with toilet training, once your dog is clean in the house, you won't need it any more. But some owners prefer to have them as a permanent fixture, especially in open-plan houses where it's harder to limit access to certain areas.

Sleeping area

This might be the same for both night-time and during the day, or your puppy might sleep in one room at night and in another when it's rest-time during the day. This means you may need two crates, or two ways of creating confinement. But wherever their base is going to be, it should be really comfortable, and promote calmness and sleep. So, you can include a soft bed, extra towels that they can move around for added comfort or snuggle under. If using a crate, you can drape a blanket over the top to make it den-like, and cut down on draughts and excess sounds. There should also be a rule that once your puppy is resting in this place, they should not be disturbed – it's very important for puppies to feel secure, and not to always be desperate to get out as soon as there's activity going on nearby.

If you're expecting your puppy to cope on their own while you leave the house, you need to teach them that being left is okay. Ideally, they should be tired before they go in their crate/ pen/ room, so they will settle more easily (e.g. after a walk, playtime in the garden or some training). They may need a chew or chew toy, to help them settle; and you can leave the radio on so the house doesn't sound so quiet. Leave without a fuss, and return in a calm way, not immediately interacting with your puppy (apart from letting them into the garden for a wee). If you act worried about leaving them, or spend too much time with them right before you head out, or have an exciting reunion when you return…all these things can make it harder for your puppy to settle on their own.

Chill-out zone

When your puppy is over-tired or is becoming hard to handle, you need to be able to put them somewhere safe where they can settle, without them biting you or other family members. Once they're over-tired or over-stimulated it's not possible to train them, because they can't think straight – they're just reacting on emotion. Once they've had a bit of chill time, you can let them back out again. You don't have to leave the room, but keep them in the crate etc long enough for them to calm down and properly relax.

Safety area

There will be moments when leaving them unsupervised could end up with them hurting themselves (e.g. eating wires, running out the front door); upsetting other people/ animals (e.g. jumping on visitors, chasing the cat, pestering an older dog); or causing damage (e.g. ripping up cushions). Rather than risk these things happening, you can leave them in their containment area, perhaps with a food treat to keep them occupied. Ideally you need to plan ahead so that they've had some activity before they go in there. Otherwise, if they're full of energy, they may get frustrated and start to bark, or chew and dig at the barrier. You can also create a pen in the garden to contain your puppy in a certain area, or you can fence off a no-go zone (e.g. if there's a hole in the fence, or there are poisonous plants you don't want them chewing).

Their happy place

Puppies need things to do in their crate, pen or room, especially when they're being left alone. You could leave them with toys, chew toys, a Kong stuffed with wet puppy food, or a treat ball with dry food in it. Anything you leave them with needs to be safe for them – make sure you've supervised them previously so you know what they're likely to do. Some puppies can be left with rawhide treats as they just nibble at them and throw them around; whereas other puppies might try to swallow big chunks whole, which wouldn't be good.

If they don't feel confident on their own, or have too much energy, or they get scared about something, or feel they are missing out on activity elsewhere in the house, they might start barking, whining, crying, or biting the bars to try and escape. Leaving a TV or radio on may help your puppy to settle quicker. They will gradually calm down, and probably go to sleep. It's a good idea to shut them in their crate or room for lots of short periods of time during the day, so that they learn how to be independent (playing and resting on their own), and how to cope with separation (dogs are social animals and would much rather be with us).

If your puppy cries with fear when they're left alone, you'll have to do some specific training with them to lessen their separation anxiety. You will also have to ignore them more when they're out of their crate as well - just come and go in the house or garden without talking to them, so they realise you're not always 'available'. They will begin to learn that there's nothing to worry about if you pop out the room for a few minutes. However, severe and longstanding cases of separation anxiety may require help from a trainer or behaviourist.

Time-out

When puppies start biting with more force, or have stopped listening when you try to distract them with toys or treats, you can use time-out (a bit like using a 'naughty step' for young children). You might put them in their crate or pen and shut the door (but don't leave them), or you can remove them from the room they're in and shut the door with them on the other side (as long as it's safe to do so). You are making it clear that there are rules to social time - they have to play nice and listen to requests.

Time-outs should be very short, just long enough to let your puppy know what the consequences of not listening to you are: up to 30 seconds is usually effective. When they're sitting quietly, let them out their crate/ pen or let them back in the room, and carry on as if nothing had happened. Be ready to do another time-out if needed. If they get worse, it's probably because they're over-tired and need a sleep, so change the crate to a chill-out zone instead and leave them there for longer (provided they've had a toilet opportunity first). Once they've had a snooze, they should be more trainable!

An aid to toilet training

Most dogs will try to avoid toileting in their sleeping area, so small crates can work well. However, it will only continue to work if you let your puppy out whenever they need to toilet, or they'll have no option but to soil their own bed (which can set up a bad habit). Large crates can have a bed at one end with a puppy pad the other, so although it's preferable to let them out to wee and poo, at least they won't be toileting on their bed. Pens can contain a small crate for sleeping, and the rest of the area is for playing, with the furthest point from the bed used as the 'toilet zone' with pads or paper. Lastly, baby gates prevent them from weeing and pooing in the rest of the house (use pads or paper by doorways if you're unable to get them outside regularly).

Even if you use containment to prevent mistakes, make sure you get them into the garden regularly when they're awake (e.g. every 20-30mins). They need plenty of opportunities to be rewarded for toileting outside, in order to set up a good habit.

Schedules

Although puppies need to know how to adapt to changes, a stable routine is important, especially when teaching them skills like house-training. Planning when to train them, play with them, groom them, walk them, and take them into the garden for toiling is an essential part of our lives with puppies. Some routines work better than others, so you will need to tweak them over time, to find what works for you and your puppy. A good way to discover that (particularly in busy households), is to keep a daily record of successes and failures.

Toileting

Puppies need to be taken into the garden regularly. When your puppy wees or poos in the garden, you need to reward them with verbal praise and a tasty food treat. If they have accidents in the house, clean it up well, and try and work out why it happened. Keeping records, both of planned trips and accidents (what was produced, where, and when), will enable you to see patterns in their behaviour, and make it easier for you to predict when they need to go out.

Playtime

Good play (i.e. fun but with rules) helps with all aspects of training and behaviour, with the added bonus that it will create a stronger bond between you and your puppy. Playtime is also training time: to teach your puppy to fetch items and give them to you, to come when you call, and to play tug nicely (to drop items when asked, and to enjoy playing so it's not about 'winning'). Puppies need lots of playtimes during the day.

Rest

Undisturbed rest and sleep are vital for a puppy's wellbeing. They learn while they're sleeping (the pathways in their brain change and strengthen, depending on what they did in the time between their last sleep and the current one); and they will be in a better mindset when they wake up (calmer, and receptive to being trained). A puppy that's overtired, or has their rest regularly disturbed, will have erratic behaviour that heads quickly towards frustration and aggression; and their increased stress levels will make it harder for them to learn, and may bring with it health issues like digestive upsets. It's important that the 'do not disturb' rule is followed by all members of the family (and visitors), which is where containment is really useful. It's much easier to enforce the 'do not disturb' rule if your puppy is safely tucked away in their pen or crate.

Sticking to the rules

Formal training with food or toys needs to happen frequently, but for short periods. During these times you need to work on basic obedience (sit, down, stand still, come, stay, leave, drop) and fun things (tricks, find the toy/ treat etc.).

General training and management (including toileting, lead walking and recall) should be constant. There is no let-up: when your puppy is awake *they are learning*, so you need to ensure they're learning the *right* things.

When you set up rules for your puppy, the whole family must agree to implement them. You could even write them down and stick them on the wall. If your puppy is going to be a well-behaved adult dog, they need to learn that they can't always do what they want, when they want. If they can see you as the bringer of good times and rewards, they will be more willing to do things for you.

When you, other family members *and* visitors have an active part in their training and behaviour management, your puppy will *always* be monitored, allowing for speedy reactions to reward or correct their behaviour. Without rules and boundaries, your puppy won't learn how to deal with frustration, and won't be able to cope without you.

'Silly time'

Although rules are important, try not to get so carried away with enforcing those rules that you forget to have fun with your puppy! Sometimes it's good for them (and us) to let off steam and go wild, for a bit of 'silly time'. Of course, if you, others or your puppy are doing anything potentially unsafe, the activity needs to be temporarily stopped to calm things down, before it begins again. There's always a moment or two during the day where your puppy will get the 'zoomies', and run round by themselves, but 'silly time' should be a moment you can *both* share.

Pushing the Reset Button

Although puppies arrive (broadly speaking) as a blank slate, problems may only become apparent after a few weeks or months. This happens either because issues develop as they grow up (when they had none initially), or because they *did* have an underlying issue but it has grown in intensity over time.Once you've decided to do something about it, and have a plan, then it's time to hit the *reset button* and start again. This can happen at any time, but a good moment is when they've returned from being neutered. As they recover, you can instil the good behaviours you had been hoping for – ones that will replace the old habits, as long as you are encouraging and consistent.

You can also push the reset button with rescue dogs. Although they come with a history, and it's important to know as much about them as you can (including their likes and dislikes), it's also important to start as you mean to go on. The first three weeks in a new home is when a rescue puppy adapts to their new environment – the people/ animals/ things/ sounds etc, and how to react to them. Help them gain confidence, and lay down the rules you want them to live by. This will make for a smooth transition. The temptation is often to let them 'settle in' by themselves, doing whatever they want to do, and *then* attempt to train them a few weeks or months later. By which time they may have learnt some undesirable behaviours, which will be harder to fix.

Whatever the problem, or whatever the plan you come up with, puppies always need your *time, attention and patience*. The more time you spend training your puppy now, the easier it becomes later.

Training Techniques

Reward-based training

If you reward your puppy when they do something you like, they will learn that it's a good behaviour to repeat. It's important that the rewards you choose are actually rewarding to your puppy – if the incentive isn't strong enough, they won't see the benefit of doing what you ask. For example, if you're teaching your puppy to do a recall, but all that's on offer is a quick pat, and possibly a single piece of their normal food, they may choose to carry on running around next time. But if the reward is lots of excited verbal praise, and a bit of cooked chicken, then they might decide it's much better to run back to you when you call them. Although we like to think our puppies will just do what we say because we ask them, and love them, the reality isn't always like that!

Rewards should be used a lot when teaching a puppy new behaviours, and when expecting more from them (e.g. sitting still when someone is talking to them). Once they have developed good habits, the quantity of rewards can be reduced. But you should keep going with your verbal praise and the occasional food reward, to 'top up' their correct responses. Ideally your puppy will become motivated to please you, and will find this rewarding by itself, which is where relationship-based training comes into its own (see below).

Focusing on rewarding good behaviours means you will be encouraging your puppy to make better choices, and to overcome any fears or difficulties they have. Once a puppy becomes afraid or angry about something, it becomes hardwired in their brain. This means that next time they see (or hear) their trigger, they react without thinking. Reward-based training helps to overwrite these associations without you having to resort to punishment (telling them off) or flooding (pushing them to cope in stressful situations). Through counter-conditioning you can teach your puppy that a previously scary event is actually a chance to earn praise and food treats. Over time, and through many repetitions, your puppy will become more confident.

The joy of using positive reinforcement (giving them rewards to increase the likelihood a behaviour will be repeated) is that it's so adaptable. *Anything* can be trained using rewards, you just need to be creative in how you present the training session. Think about how to break up big behaviours into small, easily achievable steps. For example, if you want your puppy to be able to go and lay in their bed on cue, the first thing you need to check is if they understand the 'down' cue. From there you can teach them what 'go to your bed' means. Then send them to their bed from further away, until they can do the whole sequence in one go. Any behaviour can be broken down like this, even ones that involve anxiety – just keep them in a state where they are *thinking* rather than *reacting*. Puppies who are afraid or angry won't be able to learn effectively.

Some trainers use clicker training, which uses a sound to bridge the gap between the desired behaviour being performed, and the food reward being delivered. If you want to do advanced behaviours with your puppy, or you're really interested in how far you can take reward-based training, then you might like to do a bit of research about clicker training. There are plenty of books and internet sites available to help you.

Interestingly, reward-based training isn't always rewarding. Sometimes it's about *withholding* rewards until your puppy offers a particular behaviour. So, if they're barking at you for attention, you don't want to give them a reward *until* they're quiet. Because you are taking away their chance of something nice, it's termed negative punishment. By removing or withholding a reward, the behaviour you *don't want* will *decrease.* It's a very useful technique to be aware of, but it can be a frustrating experience for puppies (and owners!) so it's best to concentrate on dishing out rewards for behaviours you want to increase, before your puppy has chance to offer a behaviour you don't want.

Relationship-based

Once you have developed a good relationship with your puppy, and they realise you are the bringer of wonderful things (attention, play, food, fun, walks etc) you can use that to help you enforce the rules, as well as to reward them when they do the right thing. It's important to use your voice and body language a lot, and remain consistent with the messages you are trying to get across. Your puppy needs to be clear when you are happy with their behaviour, and when you're not. Although it's important to have a few clear cues and commands, don't be afraid to train your puppy in a conversational way. This means they will pick up on many more cues, and dogs are capable of learning a very long list of associations.

If your body language, and your tone of voice match what you are saying, your puppy will believe what you are telling them, and will hopefully comply. But if you are saying 'no' without physically blocking them, or you're saying 'no' in a tiny, worried voice, then they know there's *wiggle room* in their behaviour. In other words, they will be testing what they can get away with. 'No' should mean 'no', so make sure you're clear about this. 'Yes' should also mean 'yes', so don't be afraid to be enthusiastic when they get something right. It's all too easy to forget about our puppies when they're being good, only to notice them when they're doing things that annoy or upset us.

Relationship-based training, when done well, reduces the need for punishment. If you and your puppy act like a team, and you are the leader of that team, your displeasure if they're getting something wrong will be keenly felt and understood by your puppy. They will want to see you smiling again, and you'll be able to help them change their behaviour into something you *can* reward. This technique is even more important when you have more than one dog, since you will have to be in charge of the 'pack'. That doesn't mean being a tyrant, but it does means guiding and shaping the behaviour of all your dogs, until you're working as a cohesive and happy unit.

Balanced training

Life is often about balance, and training is no different. It incorporates both reward-based and relationship-based training. Balanced training involves working on *three* strategies, usually all at the same time: rewards, prevention and correction. Ideally you need to *reward your puppy's good behaviour*. This might involve giving them treats, or playing with toys…and will definitely include verbal praise. Rewards are designed to encourage the *repetition* of any behaviour you want to see more of e.g. coming when called, sitting quietly, walking nicely on the lead, not scavenging, and greeting people calmly. We can't always make time to train, and circumstances mean it's not always possible. But we can still make sure that our puppies aren't learning any bad behaviours, through the use of *prevention*. Examples of prevention include: the use of collars/ leads/ harnesses/ head halters; barriers and containment; preventing access to your puppy by other people and animals; and through careful planning and management of situations (especially around your puppy's triggers). Although prevention won't teach them to do the right thing, it will stop them practising doing the *wrong* thing.

But what if your puppy is actively displaying a behaviour you think is unsafe? Or what if they're doing something that needs to be challenged immediately, so they don't think it's a good thing to keep repeating? This is when *correction* becomes necessary. But you can still be effective with even small corrections – you don't need to use lots of physical force, and you shouldn't need to shout or swear at your puppy. It's about being assertive, and making sure your body language matches what you're saying. If you want your puppy to 'leave' something, say 'leave' clearly and with meaning, and make sure you're holding your body in a confident way. If you want to stop your puppy lunging at bikes or cars, you'll need to use the lead to stop them doing this – the movements you make need to be clear, and be effective, and be paired with a clearly-stated command such as 'stop it'. Once they understand the message, you will only need to make tiny movements on the lead for them to respond. You can correct bad behaviour through verbal correction; withholding rewards; using negative reinforcement on their lead/ collar (e.g. pulling back if they're surging forward or being grumpy towards a dog/ person); and sometimes with a behavioural interrupter such as a loud noise.

Punishment should always be used carefully, and at the lowest level possible (whilst still being effective). Aim to focus on *rewards* and *prevention*, so you don't rely on punishment to correct bad behaviour. It's always better to teach your puppy to do the *right* thing. Youngsters are highly trainable, and any habits will have been recently formed, making them easier to undo.

Part 3: Frequently Asked Questions

Here you will find brief answers to common questions I've been asked over the years, about puppy and young dog training and behaviour. Although they will help you understand your puppy's motivation, and what you can do to improve the situation, please remember that the guidance on these pages is not tailored to you or your puppy. You may be able to adapt the advice, or you could seek expert help from a trainer or behaviourist if the issues remain.

Stealing things

Every time my puppy gets hold of something (like food or a tissue or a sock) he growls and snaps if I try to take it off him. What should I do?

The first thing to do is take a breath, and pause. The temptation is always to rush after a puppy to try and get the item back. This will either result in a chase that your puppy enjoys (meaning they'll want to do this more often); a quick swallow of whatever was in their mouth to stop you getting it (which could be dangerous); or an angry stand-off that might end up with someone being bitten. Get some treats, and approach your puppy slowly and calmly. Crouch down when you get close. Throw a treat near his front paws, and wait for him to decide what to do. When he let's go of the object to eat the treat, do not grab the object straight away. Throw another treat or two until he is beginning to relax. Then try to hand-feed him a treat. If this works, feed with one hand, while calmly removing the object with the other hand (and put it behind your back). Give him some more treats, then stand up and walk away (and quietly deal with the object without making a big deal about it). Although you may feel it's counterintuitive to reward him with food for bad behaviour, you have to keep in mind that you are rewarding a *de-escalation* of emotion, and the *relinquishing* of an object your puppy would much rather keep hold of.

Guarding doorways

My puppy stands in our way, in doorways, or half way up the stairs. She growls and barks, and actually looks really scary. Telling her off just makes things worse. Will she ever go back to the sweet puppy we started with?

It can be very upsetting to be confronted with an angry dog, who has learnt to control your behaviour. The thing to remember is that she's growing up fast, and her body and mind are telling her that she needs to find ways to be comfortable in her environment. Anger usually stems from feeling vulnerable about something. If she's feeling anxious about people moving around the house and leaving her on her own, she's more likely to try and prevent that movement. If she's denied access somewhere she thinks might be a good place to be (e.g. upstairs) then she will try to prevent the loss that opportunity. If she's most comfortable when the house is quiet, and everyone is where they 'should' be, then she might get defensive if family members (or visitors) change the situation by moving around. The main thing to address is her underlying anxiety or frustration. Continuing to shout at her, or punish her, will inadvertently make things worse – because it will increase her anxiety, and therefore increase the likelihood she will try to control the movements of people in the house. Use food and praise to teach her to move out of your way, or encourage her to stay in her beds (have several dotted around the house). Ask her to join you if you are moving room, or going in and out the garden. If you don't want her upstairs, fix a baby gate in place, so that she doesn't have the opportunity to go there. Once you've completed more training, and her behaviour is stable, you might be able to remove it. She's maturing, so she won't go back to the puppy she once was – you need to help her develop into a sweet *adult* dog instead!

Rough play

I don't think my puppy would really hurt another dog, but he's getting so rough with them. It's almost like he's turned into the school bully. Should I be worried?

Yes, I think it's sensible to be worried. You've realised that his behaviour is negatively affecting the dogs he's interacting with, and you would like him to behave in a more sociable way. The first thing you can do is to prevent him from having free access to dogs he's likely to get rough with (this may be all dogs at first). If he's off lead and running round, it's very hard for you to intervene. When he meets a dog on lead, you need to make sure he stays calm and friendly, and doesn't try to jump on them or run into them. The more *calm interactions* he has, the more likely it will be for him to stay calm in the future. If he meets his match in a dog that is equally boisterous, and you think they both need to let off steam, then you can let them play together. But ideally stop them both when things get a bit rough. Wait about 30 seconds or so, allowing them to calm down before letting them continue.

There is a temptation to let puppies become rough with an older dog that will tell him off, but this can go wrong in so many ways. Let's say he was pinned to the ground by a big dog – he might then become afraid of big dogs in the future, and instead of just being a 'bully' in play, he might become defensive and bark at other dogs instead. You need to be your puppy's guide. This involves rewarding him for playing well, and removing him from social time when he's getting it wrong. Over time your puppy should learn to match his play style to the other dog he's playing with.

Biting in play

My puppy keeps biting me when I try to play with him. I'm using toys, but he prefers to bite my hand! Even when I just try and stoke him, he keeps chewing me. Should I walk away from him?

You don't need to walk away (unless things are really bad), because that ends your chance to teach him to do the right thing. But you will need to have a brief time-out from play e.g. by sitting back and crossing your arms. After a few seconds, pick up the toy again, and wiggle it around. If he grabs the toy with his teeth, you can keep moving the toy and have a little game of tug. Only use light pressure though - don't try to pull it out his mouth. Keep an eye on where his grip is – if it moves too close to your hand, drop that toy and pick up another one. Long toys are useful, as you can drop one end, pick up the other end, and continue playing. Your puppy needs to learn that if he uses his teeth on skin or clothes, play ends immediately; but that play will continue if he keeps his teeth on the toy. Sometimes puppies get so wound up that they're unable to make this distinction – they're just biting *anything* that moves. If this happens, give him a squeaky toy and let him run around the garden to get rid of some energy, then help him to settle in a crate or pen with a chew.

It's also important to mention that you need to be sure your puppy *wants* to play. If you're trying to provoke him into playing because you've decided that might be nice, he might actually prefer to be left in peace! In this case, the biting is a message to tell you to leave him alone (rather than it being a mistake in play).

Biting when moved

Every time I tell my puppy she can't do something (like chewing the carpet, ripping her bed, clawing at the floor), and try to move her away, she bites me. I can't just ignore her because it's getting expensive to replace the things she's damaged. Should I tell her off?

When you tell your puppy 'no', her frustration levels instantly shoot up. If you don't replace one action for another (e.g. replacing the carpet with a filled Kong), she will also feel anxious that she can't continue with what her body or mind is telling her she needs to do (e.g. to be active, to reduce stress or to chew). Put those things together, and it will come out as an angry 'you can't tell me no!'. You might feel that telling her off is the best option, but that sets up a viscous circle. You say no, so does she, you say it louder, so does she.... The best way of dealing with this is to *diffuse and distract*. Ask yourself why she's chewing the carpet, digging on the sofa, barking at a bird through the window, playing with your shoelaces, or whatever else is upsetting you. Is she bored? Hungry? Unable to settle? Needing to chew? Needing social time?

Although you don't want to reward bad behaviour, you do need to recognise that puppies can't always communicate to us what they're feeling, and what they need – we have to look for clues in their behaviour. Ideally you want to anticipate problems, and give her a chew *before* she starts on the carpet. Or give her a walk *before* she starts winding you up. Or do some brain training exercises which will help her settle in her crate and go to sleep. If she's doing the wrong thing, call her to you, move her somewhere else (use a food treat if you need to), and reward her for doing the *right* thing. If you don't, she will simply go back to whatever it was she was doing, and the arguments will start again.

Aggression when approached

I don't think my puppy is aggressive, but if the kids stroke her when she's asleep, she wakes up and bites them, or growls at them until they go away. I want to tell her off for doing this – but is this the right thing to do?

Think about things from your puppy's perspective. She's having a lovely snooze, and suddenly she's woken up. I think that might make me a bit grumpy too. It will also make her feel insecure about her bed, as it's no longer a 'safe zone' to relax in. Although you might feel like telling her off, that could make things worse, as you will be making her feel even more upset than she already was i.e. not only has she been woken up suddenly (and potentially roughly) but now she's being told off too. The best thing to do for now is to have a very clear rule that no one should touch her while she's sleeping, or even when she's just resting. If she's awake, you (or your children) can call her over, and then start interacting with her. If she chooses to stay where she is, then leave her alone for a bit longer. Doing this means when it *is* cuddle time, or play time, she and the children will enjoy their moments together.

The only caveat with this advice is if she's on the sofa, and the kids try to sit on it too, and *then* get growled at (without them doing anything to upset her, other than trying to share the space). In this instance, you can give a firm 'off' cue, and ask her to settle on the floor or her bed instead. Don't physically move her (or you will escalate her emotions): you may have to stand your ground and be patient, but she will eventually move where you ask her to. When she has had chance to reconsider, the kids can invite her back on the sofa. This means she'll learn she can't take over or 'own' certain spaces within the house. If she becomes protective over her bed, get her accustomed to sleeping in a crate, and make sure you position it well away from the action so she can learn to settle in a relaxed state. Once she feels safe, the grumpiness should dissipate over time.

Not coming back when called

If we're in our house, my puppy comes to me when I call her. But as soon as we're outside she won't listen. She chases anything in sight, rushes into hedges where I can't see her, and sometimes runs for long distances. It's very stressful taking her for walks. How can I persuade her to come back to me?

Your puppy is more likely to listen to you at home, because there are relatively few distractions. Once you're outside however, there's a whole world of sounds, smells, and fast-moving things to investigate. If she thinks coming back to you means an end to her fun, then she's much more likely to ignore you, and carry on running around. The first thing to do is walk her on a long lead, so you can control where she goes. This also means that when you call her, you can insist she comes back by gently pulling the lead. When she does return, make sure you give her a tasty treat. Keep repeating this exercise until she's happily trotting back to you for her reward. Once you choose to let her off the lead again, do it in a safe place (well away from roads and other hazards). Don't call her back too often, or she'll get bored. But every time she responds well, give her lots of verbal praise and tasty food treats. While things are still working, pop her back on the long lead, and continue your walk, allowing her a bit of freedom to sniff and meet dogs etc (without having the chance to run off).

If your puppy loves to play, use a ball or tug toy as the reward. Get her so enthusiastic about playing with you, that she forgets her love of chasing leaves and squirrels.

If she gets it wrong, and doesn't come back to you straight away, or runs off a bit too far, avoid the temptation to tell her off when she finally returns. Although you will have become anxious or annoyed at her behaviour, telling her off will actually make things worse. Dogs are less likely to return if they know they'll get shouted at. Be happy that she's back, and give her lots of verbal praise (even if you choose to hold back the food treat until she completes a good recall). It takes lots of practise to create a reliable behaviour.

Other dogs are more fun than me

I know my puppy needs to play and socialise with other dogs, but he's so keen to do this that he won't leave them alone, and won't come back to me, or walk nicely on the lead. Does he need more time with other dogs?

This is a tricky one, because although he needs to play and socialise with other dogs, if you let him do this all the time (without there being any rules), his behaviour will become worse rather than better. You want to use the chance to play with other dogs as a reward for good behaviour e.g. listening to you, walking well on a lead, and coming back when he's called. Train these important skills when you are in an area free from distractions. Then try them out when there are dogs playing in the distance. When you are close enough that he could play with them (and it's safe to do so), ask him to sit quietly and wait for you to release him (use a cue like 'go play'). If he starts jumping around, biting the lead, or barking at you or the other dogs, simply walk him away from the action. If you are consistent with this, he will learn very quickly that he only gets to play if he follows the rules.

Refusing to come in

My puppy won't come in from the garden. It's worse when I've got to get to work. She just stands there, and sometimes she barks at me. If I try to get to her, she just runs away and I have to chase her round the garden. How can I make her come back into the house?

From her point of view, she can't understand *why* she has to come back in. She's learnt to use a couple of strategies to keep you out there for longer. Firstly, by refusing to go into the house, and also by shouting at you to join her in the garden. The other strategy is to get you to play a game with her – the game of chase. Which is a game you are unlikely to win. The more you chase, the more excited she'll get, and the less likely she'll be to want to go into the house.

At times when you have the opportunity to train her, practise recall to a food treat – anywhere in the garden, and then from the garden into the house. Always give a tasty food reward and lots of verbal praise. Then start encouraging her to go to a particular place in the house when you call her in e.g. her bed, or a mat by the door (useful on wet days). She must stay in this place for a few seconds, giving you a chance to shut the door, and *then* give her the reward. Resist the temptation to lure here there – she has to choose to complete the task. Giving her a special reward, a jackpot (multiple treats at once), or a different type of treat will help her to realise that going into the house is a *great* thing to do.

Before the training has caught up with real life, make sure you don't run out of time. Being time-pressured is the quickest route to bad feelings between puppy and owner! Perhaps you could build in time earlier in the day to play with her in the garden, so that when it's a quick visit to have a wee before you need to leave her, take her out *on a lead*. That way she won't have the opportunity to run around and refuse to go in.

Only play chase games at specific times, and with a specific cue such as 'I'm gonna get you' said in a silly voice. If you want to approach her without starting a chase game, be calm but determined in your body language, and walk slowly towards her. She'll soon learn the difference.

Jumping up

Whenever anyone shows even the slightest interest in my puppy, he jumps up at them. Not just once, but he bounces and jumps at them constantly. He won't stop. He does it in the house too. How do I stop him?

Unless you teach him what you *want* him to do (probably to sit quietly or at least have all four paws on the ground), he will carry on with what currently works (for him). Bouncing up and down is intrinsically motivating for puppies – it feels good, is exciting, and if they get attention from the person they're jumping on, then that's even better. This means they'll keep doing it, and get better at doing it: learning to jump higher, faster, with more force. If your puppy is jumping up at you, or another family member, you (or they) need to stand still and act either stern or disinterested (depending what has more effect on your puppy's behaviour). As soon as your puppy stops jumping, tell him he's a good boy, and bend down to stroke him. Only give praise and fuss if he can keep all four paws on the ground. If he's in a wild mood, give him a squeaky toy and let him run round the garden to let off a bit of steam.

If you are meeting people on walks, keep your puppy on a lead, and stop him from approaching people until he's calm. If he jumps up, move him away, and try again. Tell the other person that you're training him not to jump up, and ask that they only talk to him and stroke him if he's able to sit still (or at least not jump up). Or you could give them a treat to hand to your puppy if he sits. If they really want to say hello to him, and he can't help but jump, crouch down with him, and hold onto his collar. Don't allow him to jump and experience what a wonderful sensation it is!

The combination of prevention, withholding attention until he's getting it right, and giving him treats for sitting still will mean he'll begin to jump less. But this will need careful management for several months – if he's given the chance to jump, or is rewarded for doing so, this is a behaviour that will quickly return.

Sleeping on the sofa

We all agreed that our puppy wouldn't be allowed on the bed, or the sofa, but he keeps trying to get on them. He doesn't listen to us when we say no, and he's started showing his teeth at us if we try to push him off. What should we do?

The first thing to do is decide what you *really* want your rule to be, and why. Most of the time it's nice to share our space, and our furniture, with our dogs. It's a lovely feeling to snuggle up together on the sofa or bed, and enjoy that close friendship. Just letting a dog onto your furniture won't make them 'dominant' (which was the thinking a few decades ago). However, the guarding you are experiencing needs to be addressed. Although it's great to share with our dogs, it's important they *can* share, and don't learn that they can control the movement of people in the house through growling and snapping.

It's possible that you have inadvertently caused the issued by being forceful in trying to get your puppy to adhere to your 'no furniture' rule. If, for instance, your puppy had clambered onto the sofa while no one was looking, and had sunk into a wonderful sleep, but the next thing they knew they were being turfed off, and told off, it would only take a few goes for them to get nervous about people being around while they're trying to sleep. This would then escalate into them becoming protective over those areas.

I suspect the growling in your case probably has its origins in feelings of anxiety and vulnerability, rather than possession aggression or 'dominance'. The way to improve your puppy's behaviour is to create a new rule e.g. allowing your puppy chance to share the sofa with you, but only if they welcome family members and visitors sitting with them. He should be as willing to jump off the sofa as he is to jump onto it, and this can be trained with treats. If he can't comply with these things, then you will need to encourage him to stay in his bed, or on the floor near your feet. Make sure there are several beds around, and that they are comfortable (so it's not such a big choice between his bed or the sofa). That means you can more easily enforce the 'no sofa' rule.

However, if he's left alone in the room with the sofa, he will still try to get on it when there's no one around (dogs are opportunists). If you really don't want him on the sofa, then you will have to consider leaving him in another room, or train him to accept being in a crate.

Walking near sheep

I've heard that farmers can shoot dogs if they chase sheep. How can I train my puppy to leave them alone?

You're right about farmers having the right to shoot dogs that chase sheep, but they also have the right to do so where there is a loose dog around their sheep, even if they're not actively chasing them. So, the best option is to *always* have your puppy on a short lead when walking near sheep. This will also help to train them to stay with you when near livestock, and you can reward them with treats for keeping their attention on you instead of the sheep. Practise attention (say their name and reward them for looking at you), loose lead walking (i.e. no pulling) and 'leave' (don't pay attention to sheep or their poo!). Reward them for staying calm. If you want to let your puppy off lead, and aren't sure if there are sheep around, the basic rule is 'don't take the risk' i.e. only let your puppy off lead in places where you are *certain* there aren't sheep, cattle, horses, deer or other livestock.

Greedy puppy

I know Labradors love their food, but my puppy is a real thief, grabbing any human food she can get her paws onto. She pulls down anything within reach on tables and worktops, and can open cupboards and even the fridge. She's made herself ill a couple of times. Is there a way to stop her being so greedy?

Some dogs (including a lot of Labradors) have a missing gene, which means they never feel 'full', so if this has a genetic base then you might not be able to stop her feeling the urge to eat. But there are certainly ways you can teach her some self-control, and with careful management from you and her other caregivers, you should be able to prevent problems in the future. The best way to overcome this issue is to see her re-training in four parts.

Do specific training sessions for *'leave' and 'stay'*, when she can earn food rewards for getting it right. Start small, and gradually make the tasks harder. Aim for at least one training session a day.

Prevention is really important. When she's on her own and not being monitored, all worksurfaces and tables must be clear of anything within reach. Put child locks on cupboards and the fridge. If you have visitors, keep her on a lead. If she has any success, she will keep trying.

If you spot her about to jump up, say a stern *'no' or 'ah-ah'*. If she resists the temptation, tell her she's a good girl. If she has already jumped up, say a stern *'off'*. If she doesn't immediately comply, approach her and repeat the word - you may have to push her away by getting your body between her and the table/ worktop. Once her feet are back on the ground tell her she's a good girl. Repeat *every* time she tries. You have to be consistent and persistent with your message.

When there is temptation around, but you're not doing a specific training session, make sure she has an *alternative* e.g. a Kong filled with wet puppy food, or a tasty chew. That way she can use her urge to eat/ chew on something more appropriate, and won't be practising the behaviour of pestering and jumping up.

Going crazy on the lead

It's fine when we let our puppy off to run in the field, but getting her to walk by my side while on lead is a nightmare. She pulls all the time, and keeps running from one side to the other and trips me up, or dashes off and hurts me. Should I just walk her off-lead?

Although I can understand the temptation to only walk your puppy off the lead, this won't give you the opportunity to teach her to walk nicely on the lead, and it will reduce the places you can walk together. It also cuts down on a lot of experiences she could have e.g. walking through a town centre to get used to seeing lots of people. When teaching puppies to walk to heel (i.e. close to your side) they need a good reason to be there. The quickest way to achieve this is to give her tasty food treats when she's in the right position. If she tries to rush ahead or pull to the side, stand still, and wait for her to get back to the correct place, so you can start rewarding her again.

If you are content for her to walk ahead of you, or wander slightly to the side to sniff interesting lampposts etc, that's okay, as you can use the environment to reward her. So, if she's walking well and not pulling you (or darting quickly from side to side) you can keep moving forward and allowing her to enjoy the scents. However, if she pulls or gets over-excited, you need to stop and stand still, and wait for her to calm down. Once she's done this, you can start walking again. If she's still struggling to get the idea, you need to use the lead as a communication tool – give a little wiggle to remind her that she's connected to you. If she slows down, that's great - you can keep walking. But if she pulls or leans into the pressure, you can try a short 'pull-back and release' to see if that works. If she rushes forward or leans into the pressure, turn around and make her walk in the opposite direction for a few paces, then try again.

The important thing to remember is *consistency*. You have to keep doing all these things, *every* time your puppy tries to race ahead, trip you up, or pull you forward (or back). Although this can seem like a never-ending task, if your timing is right, and you reward her when she starts to walk calmly, then you will have a lifetime of happy walks, both on-lead and off-lead.

Stubborn teenager

My puppy did everything I asked when he was little, but now he won't do anything I say. Sit, down, come here, leave it…it's all been forgotten. Is he just being stubborn?

He's probably just being a teenager. That doesn't give him a free pass to be naughty, and you will need to continue with his training, but it will help you understand the changes you are experiencing. When puppies are very young, they want to (and need to) seek protection from their caregivers. But once they have a bit more independence, they challenge the status quo, to see if they can control more resources. So, if you ask your puppy to lie down, and he can't see the benefit of doing it, he may choose to not do that. He's waiting to see what your reaction is. If you give up, he'll know he doesn't have to comply with what you're asking him to do. Which might not be a problem for a simple lie down, but it might become a problem with other things e.g. recall. The other aspect of puppies becoming teenagers is that their brains are rewiring – they are learning and relearning so much that sometimes the connections between cues and behaviours get a bit tangled, or lost. Which means things they used to do easily can suddenly be met with a confused expression. They don't comply because they can't remember *how* to. This usually goes in phases for several months, and you just need to keep repeating their early lessons until all the pieces fit back into place. Avoid the temptation to get frustrated with your puppy, or to increase your use of telling off (or other punishments). Adolescent dogs need a lot of time and patience if they are to continue learning the right behaviours, and not get stressed or anxious. If you can develop his motivation and willingness, his behaviour will stabilise as he grows up, and you will have a happy and compliant older dog.

Attention seeking

My puppy won't leave me alone. She's constantly pawing at me, or barking at me, or pushing me or bringing me toys. I've tried ignoring her but it's getting worse, and it's driving me crazy. What should I do to stop her?

Your puppy is desperate for your attention, and has learnt that these techniques work. Attention-seeking is just communication, so there will be a reason it started. Think about your puppy's daily routine, including how many walks she gets, how much play time she has, and how much training she gets. It might be that what you consider adequate for her to settle, isn't the right level of exercise or activity for her. Although I'm not suggesting you allow your puppy to dictate what happens and when, dogs usually only use attention-seeking if their needs aren't being met. For example, if you did ten minutes of brain training with her, and then a five-minute play session, she would probably be ready to settle, and you can get on with your work unimpeded. Or if you only walk her twice a day, perhaps she needs the mental and physical stimulation of going out three times a day instead, perhaps to different places. They don't have to be long walks – just interesting ones!

Once you've made a few changes to her general management and routines, you can then tackle her annoying habits. So, if she's pawing at you, tell her to lie down. Once she does this, after a few seconds, quietly tell her she's a good girl. Make sure you only give her attention if she's resting by your side or in her bed. If she needs extra information to help her make the connection, say 'no' as she paws you or tries to jump on you, then lead her out the room and shut the door. Wait two seconds, then let her back in. Remember to praise her if she does the right thing. It may be that you've become so used to only noticing her when she does something wrong, that you've forgotten to reward her when she's doing the *right* thing. This may be why ignoring her isn't working in the way you intended it to. But a few small changes should make a big difference.

Muddy puppy

When we're on a walk, my puppy seems determined to come home as dirty and smelly as possible. He runs into stagnant water, rolls in fox poo, jumps into muddy puddles, and he won't listen to me when I tell him not to. Is there any hope of keeping him clean?

There are several ways I could answer this, but the summary would be: reward him (with food, praise and games) when he steers clear of the yukky places; prevent his access to the worst bits (especially when you don't have time to clean him afterwards) by keeping him on lead or walking him in areas where he won't come across stagnant pools; and then make sure you correct his behaviour if he attempts to enter a muddy puddle or roll in something unpleasant. This last bit is only effective if you are close enough to him that you can back up your words with body language e.g. getting between him and the puddle, and telling him to move away from it. Once he's already in, it's too late to start the punishment – he's already *had* his moment of joy, and you telling him off will only be linked to recall which will make him *more* likely to run off and explore next time rather than less. So, *prevention and rewards* are the strategies you should focus on. Also, think about giving him other things to find enjoyable on a walk e.g. playing fetch or tug. If a puppy is left to their own devices, they will quickly find their own entertainment!

Endless licking

My puppy won't stop licking my hands, or the hands of anyone else she's friends with. It's a really unhygienic behaviour – how do I stop it?

This behaviour is often a sign of anxiety. She's desperate to make contact, and to demonstrate appeasement behaviour ('I'm timid and not a threat, please don't hurt me'). Which is why it's not a good idea to tell her off for doing it – this would *add* to her anxiety, creating an even stronger desire to lick/ appease. Although it's better than being ignored or being bitten, I can understand why you would prefer her not to do this! The best way is to make sure that greeting people is done in a calm and non-confrontational way, in order to take any stress out of the situation. Then verbally praise her if she copes with being stroked without her needing to lick you or others. If she tries to lick, move your hands away from her and wait a couple of seconds. Then try again. If you are consistent with this, she will learn to enjoy physical contact without needing to lick anyone. The other option is to encourage her to have a toy in her mouth when she interacts with anyone. This 'comfort blanket' will help her to stay confident, and she can be stroked without the risk of her starting to lick. Over time she will get used to the new way of greeting people.

Sore paws

Is there a way to stop my puppy licking her paws? She's making them really sore.

The first thing to do is get your puppy checked out by a vet, as there are medical conditions that can cause dogs to lick themselves excessively. A vet will also be able to investigate possible allergic reactions. If her skin is very sensitive, you may need to wash them in mild dog shampoo after walks. Once given the all clear, you could try changing her food to see if that makes a difference. Dietary allergies and intolerances can sometimes lead to skin irritation, which can result in sore paws. If you do all these things, and the situation hasn't improved, see if there's a connection between her licking her paws and the time of day, or what's happening around her. Excessive licking can become a dog's way of coping with stress when they're left alone, or if there are things happening in their environment that are out of their control (e.g. noises, smells, lots of visitors, changes of routine). Licking releases 'feel good' chemicals in the body, which can become addictive. This means that even after the original stressors have disappeared, the habit remains. So, you will have to do a bit of retraining to stop the cycle. Distraction is a great way to do this e.g. refocus the licking from her feet and onto a Kong filled with tasty food. Use lots of verbal praise to reward her as well. Anytime you see her trying to lick her feet, gently encourage her to lick the Kong (or chew) instead. Make sure you do lots of brain training with her as well, so she can settle more quickly, and fall asleep before she has chance to think about licking her feet.

Humping

My puppy is full of energy, and loves everybody. But (it's so embarrassing to admit) he keeps humping people's legs. Sometimes it's cushions and toys. It always happens more when we have visitors. He even did it to someone we met on a walk. How can I stop him?

Humping often happens when a puppy is stressed or frustrated, and doesn't know how to cope with a situation. As puppies grow up, levels of hormones fluctuate, which can also lead to humping: their bodies are getting ready for the 'real thing'! The other reason dogs might show this behaviour is to control others – often termed 'dominance' in the past, but it's a little more complicated than this. Because you say it happens more when there are visitors, or when he meets someone new, I think it's probably a spike in emotion (whether anxiety or excitement) and your puppy doesn't know how to respond. So, you need to spend time teaching him an alternative behaviour – the easiest way is to change his humping activity to a fun game of tug or fetch. It means he can still get rid of some of his emotions through movement, but it will be a bit more appropriate, and will be a behaviour you can encourage. Once you've begun this process, it's okay to give a stern 'no' if he attempts to hump a person's legs (or if he tries to hump another dog), and then move him away.

If encouraging him to play doesn't work, and he's still trying to hump, use food treats to help him concentrate on something else e.g. sitting and giving a paw, or lying in his bed. If he humps his own toys, you could just ignore it (but you need to *really* ignore him - if you watch him, or talk to him, or laugh etc then this could form part of an 'attention seeking' repertoire). Always make sure you praise the behaviour you like, and either ignore the unwanted behaviour (if there are no negative consequences) or actively discourage it. As long as you remain calm and are consistent with the messages you give your puppy, it shouldn't take long to get him over this embarrassing habit.

Scared to meet other dogs

I've had a few bad experiences in the park when dogs have rushed over to my puppy and frightened her. She's getting scared to meet other dogs now, and has started to bark at them. What can I do to get her confidence back?

It's probably a good idea at the moment to avoid walking where dogs are running off-lead. Try sticking to areas where other dogs are more under control. This means that when your puppy sees another dog, she has nothing to fear. She's still likely to bark though, so you will need to do a bit of retraining. The best way is to use food treats when she responds to her name and looks at you, or walks away from things that worry her. If she's able to watch another dog without barking, use lots of verbal praise to encourage her when dogs are a long way away, and to reassure her that everything's going to be okay. If the other dog is approaching you, keep a very close eye on her body language. If her body becomes tense, or you see frown lines appearing on her head, or if the lead goes tight…it means her emotions are building.

If you stay where you are, pretty soon she'll stop coping, and start barking. So, move away while things are still working e.g. say a cheerful 'let's go!' or 'this way!' and move away from the other dog. If she's able to stay still for longer, and the other dog is calm and friendly, you may be able to get close enough for her to make friends. If she's able to do this that's great – use lots of verbal praise to encourage her, and keep the lead loose. But always be ready to move her out of trouble if she gets worried, or if the other dog gets excited (or grumpy). Always aim to interrupt her before things escalate. Once she's coping meeting dogs in this way, you can go back to off-lead parks and see if you can put your training into action there. The other good thing to do is arrange puppy play dates with other puppies, so she can develop her social skills and learn that it's fun to greet other dogs, and to play with them.

Competitive barking

I have two puppies from the same litter, and if one barks at another dog on a walk, the other one barks too, and then they get louder and more aggressive-sounding. But I think they're actually worried. What should I do?

It's harder when you have two dogs, because it's tricky to get the timing right when training both together. So it's a good idea to do separate walks at first, allowing you to concentrate on one at a time. Reward when they respond to their name, when they stay quiet, and when they willingly walk away from a situation when you ask them to. Also make sure they aren't pulling on the lead, as this will quickly lead to an increase in emotion if they see one of their triggers (another dog). Once they're behaving well on their own, take them both out together, and continue your training. You will find you won't be able to get as close to their triggers at first, and that's okay – continue to reward good behaviour from a distance. If one starts barking, you need to say a stern 'no' or 'enough', then reward them if they're quiet. If both start barking, direct the words to both of them. If they won't be quiet, use the leads to get them to step back from the trigger (make sure the lead is slack once they have done this – constant pressure will build emotion). If they can't do this, then move them away from the situation and calm them down before reapproaching. You are bound to have a few setbacks, but remain determined to sort it out – your dogs will be looking to you for guidance. If you feel in control, they will accept and respond to your guidance. After all, at the moment, they *think* they are doing the right thing.

Hiding under the table

Walking is supposed to be fun, but when I try to take my puppy out, she hides under the table and won't come out for me to put her harness on. She does it when people visit as well, and she won't say hello to them. Why is she doing this?

She's telling you she's worried about something. By hiding away she's avoiding having to meet your visitors, is avoiding having to go into the big scary world outside, and is avoiding the potential discomfort of the harness being fitted. Although you may never work out what caused this anxiety in the first place, you need to help her learn that things aren't *really* that scary. Avoid the temptation to force her to talk to people, or force her to go on a walk, as this will likely create more resistance on her part, and does nothing to convince her that these things can be pleasurable. If she hides when people come into the house, just let her do this at the moment. As long as she's not growling when she's there, leaving her alone will allow her to calm down. If she does appear, scatter a few treats on the floor – but remind your visitors to ignore her. She will make friends with them when she feels more secure.

But going out on walks is a really important part of a dog's life, and puppies need to go out to learn about the world, which means this issue *has* to be tackled. First, use treats and praise to ensure you can put on a simple collar and lead without her getting worried. If you prefer to use a harness, choose one that you can clip over her back rather than one you push her head through. Train her in the house and garden to walk nicely on the lead, to sit when asked, and to respond to her name by looking at you. Then work by the front door…then the path and front garden/ drive…then along the pavement. Keep a close eye on her body language – you want her to be keen to learn, rather than terrified and desperate to get back home. See if you can get a bit further on each walk, using lots of tasty treats when she gets something right (e.g. sitting, walking with you, coming to you when you say her name). When she can happily leave the house and walk several meters away from the house, you can keep walking, or pop her in the car and take her somewhere else (but make sure she will enjoy it – don't take her anywhere too busy where she might get scared by people, traffic, noises etc). If she gets scared on a walk, support her in that place (if it's safe to do so) until she's able to realise that she's okay, and can continue. Desensitisation takes time, but if done carefully, she will soon learn that walks are a fun part of life.

Over-sensitive

My puppy is so sensitive that he won't let me brush him, or put a collar on him. The day we managed to put a lead on him he screamed until we took it off again. Is this normal?

This over-reaction is normal for a sensitive puppy who hasn't learnt that it's okay to have a collar on, and that it's pleasurable to be brushed. You will need to start at the beginning, and build his confidence up. If he accepts you cuddling him, and making a fuss of him, you can start grooming him in your arms. But you mustn't restrain him, or do anything that will upset him – start very slowly with a soft brush. Do a couple of strokes, then give him a little food treat. Talk to him all the time about how clever he's being. If things get too much for him, or you've pushed things too far, pop him on the floor and leave him alone for a minute or two. Then see if he'd like to try again – hopefully his enjoyment of attention, cuddles and treats will help him get over his fears. Once he's coping with this, you can groom him while he's on the floor, or suitable non-slip surface, and get him used to different brushes and combs. If he's a breed that will need to be clipped or bathed regularly, get him used to this too, or his first visit to the groomers will be very traumatic for him. The collar going on should be part of a training plan to get him used to being touched all over, and held/ restrained. He also needs to get used to the idea of moving away from pressure – so if you gently pull his collar towards you, and he feels that pressure on his neck, he should come *towards* you. A panicking puppy will try to run away from pressure, which of course increases the pressure and makes the panic worse. Use tasty food treats to get him used to these sensations. Only take him out for a walk once he's fully accepting the collar and lead in the house and garden – you don't want him panicking outside, or he will learn to be afraid of a much longer list of things!

Scared of cars

My puppy is so scared about cars that he won't walk anywhere, and looks so terrified all the time. How can we make walks more fun for him?

Although you need to get him used to the sound of cars, bikes and lorries, you also need to convince him that walks are usually fun. So for a week or two, only walk in quiet areas where he can learn to relax and enjoy himself. Then you can put a training plan into action. Initially walk him far enough away from traffic that he can hear it, but not be too upset about it. Give him lots of encouragement with verbal praise and the odd tasty treat. Gradually get closer to the traffic. While he's still coping move further away again, and have a breather, before starting the next attempt to get closer. The aim is to keep him calm and learning – he won't be able to learn once he's scared or stressed. If there's a loud noise that troubles him, try to time the treat so you reward him when he hears the sound but before he's had chance to become scared by it. This is called counter-conditioning: when the *opposite* thing happens to what he's expecting. So instead of a motorbike roaring past being linked to feeling scared, it becomes a chance to eat sausages (for example). Some dogs prefer to move when they're a bit nervous (to use up the adrenaline that's been released), others prefer to stand or sit still and work things out. Go at the pace your puppy can cope with – pay close attention to his body language. Reward him when he's calm and coping. If he looks terrified then you're too close to his triggers, and you'll need to do a bit more training further away.

Terrified of brooms

My puppy is terrified of me doing housework. He used to run away, but now he tries to attack brooms, brushes, mops, the vacuum cleaner and even the feather duster. I've started to shut him away, but he still barks. Is it possible to get him used to all this?

As a quick answer, yes it is…with some training and desensitisation. At the moment he thinks these things are dangerous, and are a threat to you as well as him. So when you shut him away, he's desperate to get out and protect you. Depending how this behaviour first started, or what happened when it changed from 'running away' to 'attacking', there's a chance that he's no longer scared of the cleaning equipment, and is actually having fun trying to grab them. In other words, it might have become a game. But the way forward is the same whether he's afraid or over-excited. When you start your training, have plenty of tasty food treats handy. Place the problematic items on the floor, and reward him for staying calm while walking near them and sniffing them, and then when you carefully pick them up. Once this is working, start moving the items around. Continue to reward for calm behaviour. If he starts barking, or rushes towards something, say a stern 'no' or 'enough' and wait for him to stop. If he doesn't, tell him to leave the room, or at least back off a bit. Avoid the temptation to send him to his bed, because you want him to feel comfortable there, and not stressed. After a few seconds, ask him to come back to you. Then you can resume the training, but only at a level he can cope with. Gradually get him to walk with you round the house, following the mop or broom, or lying on the ground next to you while you use a dustpan and brush, or the duster. Keep talking to him while he's coping – reward his good behaviour with attention.

Desensitisation to the vacuum cleaner may take longer as it involves noise, but the principle is still the same. Once it's switched on, as far away from him as necessary, gradually get closer until you can switch it on and off while he's fairly close. You can throw the treats from a distance. Get him used to moving away from the vacuum cleaner, and plan your routine so he can be in one room while you clean another. When it's time to swap, turn the vacuum cleaner off, move him into another room, and then carry on with your housework. By doing this you are helping him predict what's going to happen and when, and he will feel more able to cope.

Separation anxiety

I can't leave my puppy alone, even for a few seconds. He howls, cries, barks, and scratches the door. It's horrible to hear him like this. But I have to go out sometimes – what can I do to help him cope?

This sounds like separation anxiety, meaning your puppy can't cope without you. As it's an issue that can take a little while to fix, it's best if you can find someone to look after your puppy when you have to go out. You could sign them up for doggy day-care, or have a friend sit with them to help them cope. This means it won't undo any training you do with him on the days you're home.

Part of the training involves teaching him how to stay in his bed (or on the sofa), and remain calm until you return. This starts as a simple sit-stay, and then you can gradually increase the time he can wait, and the distance you can walk away. If he can't even cope being left for ten seconds before barking, or rushing towards you, then you will have to do a lot more work at this level. Only give him a treat if he hasn't moved from where you left him, and if he stays calm on your approach. If he jumps up or gets excited, you need to start again. Although you can say a calm 'good boy' as you walk towards him, avoid sounding too excited or it will be harder for him to stay still. Once you can be out of sight for a minute, you are making progress. Then, rather than it being a formal stay, you need to come and go without announcing you're leaving. But don't stay away for longer than your puppy can cope with – initially this will only be a few seconds. Very gradually, you'll be able to get to five minutes or more. Leave without fussing him, or talking to him…and return the same way. Don't make eye contact, don't talk to him or stroke him. Just wander past and make a mug of tea, or flick through a magazine. After about a minute you can calmly talk to him, or let him in the garden for a wander (if you have left him for longer, let him in the garden straight away in case he needs a wee). The calm leavings and calm returns will avoid him getting excited about your return (which can significantly increase the distress puppies feel when they're on their own).

As it's usually the *leaving* that's the issue, once you've got your puppy to accept that part without becoming afraid, it usually doesn't take long to build your absence to an hour or so. But always give him something nice to eat while you're out e.g. a treasure hunt of dry food, a treat ball, or a Kong stuffed with wet puppy food. This will help distract him, and reward him for coping alone. If the food isn't eaten until you return, it's because he *hasn't* been coping, so it's a good test. The other thing you can do is set up a remote camera so you can monitor him from your phone/ tablet while you're out the house. Make sure he's had a good walk before leaving him, so he's more likely to settle. A quietly playing radio will also help him relax.

Afraid of the crate

We've tried to crate train our puppy, but she's terrified of it. We can't leave her loose in the house because she chews things and toilets inside, and chases the cats. We really need her to be used to the crate – what can we do?

It might be a good idea to get a sturdy pen to go around the crate, so that she can learn to love the crate as a place to sleep but can wander away from it to play or toilet. When getting a puppy used to a crate, it's important to make sure they enter it calmly e.g. for a food treat. When the door is shut, don't immediately leave. Talk to her quietly if she's coping – the aim is to help her learn to self-sooth so she can relax and go to sleep. The easiest way to reach this point is to make sure she's physically and mentally tired before she goes in the crate (or pen and crate). You could take her for a walk, or play with her in the garden, and do a bit of obedience training with her so she has to think lots. Once she's in the crate, give her something to chew/ lick (e.g. a Kong filled with wet puppy food) to help her while she's still feeling active. Put a radio or TV on so there is some background noise, then you can wander away, but don't go out the room until she's learning how to settle. You don't want her to panic as soon as you leave. It's also important to come back to her, and open the crate door, *before* she gets anxious. So, after a little snooze, open the door. She might choose to stay in there, which is great, or to come out – but don't give her any attention at this stage, or you'll be reinforcing her belief that being out the crate is much better than being in it. Once she can be left for half an hour, you should be able to stretch the time.

The crate should be really inviting, with a cover over it to make it den-like, and it should be large enough for your puppy to lie flat, and turn around. If you are just using a crate, it might need to be big enough to have a bed one end and a puppy pad the other (depending on how long you intend leaving her – especially at night). Because you need to teach her how to behave when loose in the house, you will also need to spend time training her not to chew things, and to not chase the cats. This will involve careful management, 'leave' training, providing alternatives (e.g. Kongs, toys, and other distractions), as well as setting up suitable barriers such as baby gates to give your cats a place of sanctuary.

Eating poo

Right from when we first had our puppy, she's been eating her own poo! We try and clear it up as soon as possible, but we don't always get there in time. It's so horrible when she then licks our children. How can we stop this?

Sometimes poo-eating is a behaviour that's learnt from when puppies are still with their littermates. It can happen in nervous puppies who don't want to announce their presence: eating their poo conceals that they're living there. If this applies to your puppy, she might appear to be a bit worried about being in the garden alone, eating her poo as soon as she goes, and she might not poo at all on a walk. If this is the case, then you'll need to increase her confidence being out, and reward her with treats for not just pooing, but for pooing and then coming back to you. This will give you enough time to clear up the waste before she thinks about eating it. You will have to monitor her carefully, and go out into the garden *every* time you suspect she might need to poo. You want to avoid her practising this behaviour.

The other main reason puppies do it is dietary. This might be because something is lacking in their diet; or through curiosity (trying out new things) that then becomes a habit. As long as your puppy is on a good quality, complete food, and doesn't suffer any intolerances or allergies, then you know she's getting all she requires. It's okay for you to say a stern 'no' or 'leave' if you see her sniffing her poo (which she will do before eating it, unless it's such a strong habit that she just wolfs it down without thinking). If you can predict you won't be quick enough to stop her, or that she will ignore anything you say or do to try and interrupt her, keep her on a lead to prevent her moving towards it. When doing 'leave' training, you need to reward compliance i.e. giving her food treats if she stay aways from the poo, or comes to you instead. Then clear up the poo so she can't rush to it when you're not looking. When out on a walk, monitor her behaviour closely (keep her on a lead), especially if she's likely to try out other dog's faeces as well.

Tasty sheep poo

My puppy leaves dog poo alone, but apparently all *other* poo is delicious. Horse, cow, sheep, cat, goose…the list seems endless. Although his recall is usually pretty good, he goes deaf when there's poo to be eaten. Please help!

From a dog's perspective poo can be potential food, and for a puppy who tries out everything, finding something with an interesting taste can quickly form into an unwanted habit. The best way to tackle this is to teach him what 'leave' means (i.e. 'don't touch it!'). You also need to work on recall, so you can call him away from a pile of poo before he has chance to get close. This is a very hard decision for a dog to make, so you'll need to keep him on lead at first. Head for areas where you know there is temptation. Keep him under control on a short lead, and start walking. If he shows interest in the poo remind him to 'leave' it. If he moves away, or focuses on you, give him a food reward. Practise loose lead walking past the poo, round it, near it and then move onto the next bit. You need to reward him for sniffing other things, or when he's happy to walk by your side without pulling. Use lots of verbal praise to encourage good behaviour, and be constantly on alert for potential issues. When this is working on a short lead, progress to an extendable lead or long training line. Prevent him achieving his goal, but try to encourage him to step away from the poo himself, then reward him with a food treat for complying. If he's being very insistent, stand between him and the poo and 'own it' i.e. be confident in your tone of voice and your body language that you *will not* let him pass. Keep telling him this until he chooses to walk away or back off, then reward him and walk away together. It takes lots of persistence to reduce this habit, but it's possible for your puppy to be able to leave poo alone even when he isn't on a lead.

Not eating enough

I'm worried that my puppy isn't eating enough food. She always seems to be on the go, but when I put her food down, she just looks at it, and won't touch it. I've tried hand feeding her, but that doesn't work either. She's getting skinny. What should I do?

The first thing you need to do is relax. If you have a sensitive dog, the more pressure you put on her, the less likely she is to eat anything. She will be able to sense your worry without understanding what you're worried about, and will assume you're concerned about the food itself, or the act of eating. It's probably a good idea to change her food, so you can start again with a new smell/ taste that she won't associate with anxiety. You can also choose something with different ingredients, in case she was experiencing digestive discomfort from the original food. Aim to choose a brand that has both wet and dry versions. The wet food can either go in a small bowl at mealtimes, or in a Kong at other times of the day. Dry food can be for mealtimes, scatter-fed for a fun treasure hunt, or used in training.

When you place a bowl down for a meal always put a lot less in there than you think she needs, and give her ten minutes to eat it. If she walks away from it during this time, simply pick up the bowl and put it in the fridge (if it includes wet food). Offer it again in a few hours. Don't look at her when you place the food – get interested in a book, or watching TV. Some puppies will eat if they are left alone, some will only eat if they have company – you will have to experiment with what works for her.

The dry biscuits can be used in a fun food game: call her to you, and as she runs over, throw a piece of food to the side. Once she's eaten it, call her to you again, and throw the next bit the other way. She will hopefully think this is fun, and eat the food without thinking about it. Only do this for a few goes, and stop while she's still enjoying it. Once she's got the idea and is happy to eat food during training, you can practise 'sit' or walking to heel as well. If she won't work for dry food in her training, you could use cooked chicken breast – at least you will know she's getting some good nutrients into her.

After several days of this new regime, she should begin to eat small amounts. It's really important you don't over-face her. Keep putting a lot less in her bowl/ Kong than you think. If she polishes it off and looks to you for more, you can add another spoonful. Do this up to two times, and then tell her it's end of food time. That way she'll be more keen next time. If you try all this and nothing seems to work, have a chat with your vet in case there's an underlying medical issue.

Eating the cat's food

My puppy keeps eating my cat's food – is this a problem? He really loves it, and the cat doesn't seem bothered.

If your cat's food is going to be available all the time, it's best to keep it out the way of your puppy (either up high, or in a room that your cat can access but your puppy can't). Dog food is designed for a dog's nutritional needs, and cat food for cats – it's best that they don't eat each other's food. Although cats would become poorly if only given dog food (because it lacks certain amino acids and has less protein content), dogs can usually eat cat food without too many negative effects. However, it can cause dietary intolerances in some dogs, leading to diarrhoea; or an increased risk of conditions of the kidney, liver and pancreas. Cat food also tends to be higher in fat and protein, which may not be ideal for the growth (and the weight) of your puppy. Dogs are attracted to cat food because it's usually 'tastier' than dog food, which means they'll binge on it if they get access to it.

If you feel bad denying your puppy the chance to eat your cat's dry food, you can always use the occasional bit as a training treat instead of cheap packaged treats (which won't be as good nutritionally). Just don't overdo it!

Crazy moments

My puppy sometimes goes crazy - running round very fast, crashing into things, and jumping onto things. It's impossible to stop her, and if I manage to get hold of her, she tries to bite me. Is this a sign of aggression?

I think your puppy is experiencing the 'zoomies' – charging around, having lots of fun, but not being fully aware of what she's doing! It's normal for puppies to do this, and it isn't a sign of aggression. She's full of energy and excitement, and it's reached such a high level that she doesn't know what to do with herself. The dashing around is her way of letting off steam. Because she can't think straight when this happens, if you try to stop her, her frustration bubbles over and she uses her teeth to try to get away and run around again.

When she's in this state it's best to leave her alone, and let her zoom round (provided it's a safe area for her to do this in). If the garden is better, then encourage her to go out there, perhaps by squeaking a toy for her to follow and then throw it for her. Don't try to train her when she's this revved-up, as she won't be able to concentrate; and don't try to pick her up. Once she's run round a few times, show her a toy and see if she'll engage in play. Or you can rustle a treat packet and encourage her to come to you for a reward.

Because she will grow bigger, and might hurt herself (or another dog or a person) or might cause damage, you will need to develop a 'stop' cue. This is especially important when she's on a lead and you can't allow her to run free, or move away from you (for example if you're near a road). Even if you get her to stop still, she will be so full of energy, and her heart rate so high, that you will have to find a way to calm her down quickly or the urge to shoot off again will be irresistibly high. You might need to hold her collar with one hand, and try to prevent her body spinning round with the other. Tell her to sit, and offer her treats once she's able to do this. Getting tangled up in a lead, or being pulled along can be dangerous. There's a time and a place for zoomies!

Hyperactivity

My puppy is constantly on the go, playing with toys, following me round, chasing birds in the garden, always ready for a walk, jumping on the kids…she never seems to settle. If she doesn't get enough sleep, she gets grumpy - but if we shut her in the crate, she bites the bars and makes her mouth sore. How can we make her settle?

There are several things going on here. You will need to assess how much quality play, training, walks and social time she's getting at the moment. This will depend on how old she is, but it's important to get her out into the world experiencing different locations, people and animals. The more she's had to learn (in particular, the more sniffing she's done), the more likely she is to settle when she gets back. Playtime needs to have a few rules so that she learns to play tug and fetch without getting overexcited or competitive (which can increase adrenaline and make it hard for her to calm down afterwards). Even if you've taught her basic obedience, don't stop training her – try more advanced things, or plan lots of tricks to teach her. The more she's had to think, the more she will enjoy her downtime. You might also want to look at the food you're giving her, as some food allergies and intolerances can result in excess energy or an inability to settle. Once all this is in place, you can then teach her how to rest by herself – either in a crate/ pen, or in a room where she can't get up to too much mischief. One way to do this is to give her a chew or a Kong filled with wet puppy food, so she can enjoy licking and chewing it, then fall asleep afterwards. Make sure there's a radio on nearby to help soothe her.

Take her out the crate/ pen/ room regularly for toileting, play, training, social time and walks. To help her not follow you around, you can teach her to stay. But if you don't mind having a shadow, it might be easier to let her follow you: just don't make a big deal about it. Acknowledge she's there, but don't talk to her or interact with her. Some dogs are more sensitive or alert than others, so if her crate is in an area where she can see things moving in the garden or in the street, or it's near where family members are constantly walking past, it might be a good idea to change location. She will gradually learn that there are times to be energetic, and times to relax – but she will only learn this if you teach her what to do.

If she's still struggling to settle, you could learn the basics of canine massage – there are techniques that will help to lower her heart rate and to encourage relaxation.

Destructive puppy

My puppy ruins any toy (and any object) he gets hold of. He shreds it, throws it around, rolls over it, and as soon as that one's 'dead' he's looking for the next thing. It's costing me so much money! How can I make him stop being so destructive?

Destructiveness can be a sign of pent-up energy or stress, so make sure he's getting out on lots of interesting walks, and you're working on his general obedience as well. Apart from finding sturdier toys (like the tougher Kongs that you can fill with wet puppy food, or strong chews that take more work before they disappear), there are several other things you can try. The first is to teach him how to play with toys without destroying them. If he learns to play fetch, he will run after the toy, perhaps shake it, but then bring it back to you for another go. Keep these sessions short so he's not tempted to find a corner of the garden to settle down and chew his prize. Exchange the toy for a food reward if necessary. Also, teach him how to play tug with toys (e.g. strong rope toys), so he can have fun pulling, but it's part of a game rather than him trying to grab it and run off with it. You should remain in control, and be able to stop play whenever you want by saying 'stop' or 'drop' – once he lets go, the game can resume with the cue 'tug-tug!'. If he doesn't want to let go of an item, use a tasty food treat. Once play time is over, collect all the toys and store them in a box in a cupboard. Only leave him with the tougher toys and chews.

The other thing you can do is accept that your puppy loves a bit of destructive play. This might just be a phase, or something he's going to enjoy even as an adult. One way to get round this is to make up treasure boxes that he can have fun ripping up. You can get cardboard boxes and, (like a pass the parcel) put treats in each layer. You can use scrunched-up paper as well to make things interesting. Make sure it's safe for your puppy, so remove all staples, tape and packing material. Always supervise him during this game, and make it very clear to him that he's allowed to destroy *this* item i.e. put it on cue, and perhaps only doing this in a specific location. This means he won't seek out *other* carboard boxes (and assume that everything's fair game) – which is where your 'leave' training comes in. By allowing outlets for his energetic behaviour, the unwanted instances will gradually lessen.

Bullying an older dog

How can I stop my puppy harassing my older dog? I know she only wants to play, but my other dog is ten and has started snapping at her. I don't want things to get worse.

You're right to be concerned about the situation getting worse, and it's not fair on your older dog either. Your puppy has a lot more energy and stamina, and will naturally be persistent in her encouragement to play. If a play bow won't work, she will try pouncing, barging, nipping, chasing etc. You need to teach her to leave your other dog alone. Stand between her and your older dog, and use the 'leave' cue or just say 'enough'. Once she moves away, verbally reward her. However, puppies will quickly go back to their previous activity if they're not redirected onto something more appropriate. If she's awake and active, you need to play with her yourself, rather than leave her to find her own amusement. Use toys to play fetch or tug, get her running round the garden, use treats to practise recall training or walking to heel. Or take her out for a training walk. If she has a strong need to play with another dog, try to arrange to meet up with suitable puppies and dogs on your walk, or for specific play dates.

At home, make sure your older dog is able to rest without interruption. This may necessitate setting up a baby gate so they can be in a separate room; or teach your puppy to settle in a crate (or a crate plus a pen). Doing this means you can supervise their time together, and can back up your older dog if they're attempting to tell your puppy to calm down or leave them alone (without them having to resort to growling and snapping).

Chasing cats

Is it normal for puppies to chase cats? Will our puppy and our two cats ever be friends?

Dogs and cats *can* be friends, but it takes a lot of training (on both sides!). The trouble is that cats are more likely to run when spooked by a dog - and dogs love to chase things that move. So, it's inevitable that dogs learn that chasing cats is a fun thing to do. You will need to teach your puppy a strong 'stay' cue, as well as 'leave'. Use lots of food treats to reward them for staying calm around your cats, and use a lead if you think your puppy can't resist trying to run after them. Make sure your cats have plenty of escape routes, especially places higher than your puppy can reach. Your cats may also need unhindered access to and from the garden through the cat-flap, which may require a bit of thought about how to keep them separate. It's best to keep your puppy on a lead in the garden if you know your cats are out there: again, work on the 'stay' and 'leave'. If your puppy gets excited or frustrated, say a stern 'no' or 'enough', and remind them what they should be doing. You will gradually be able to trust them more, but close supervision is really important. It's easier to stop an *intention* to chase, than the chase itself.

Frightened of a baby

There's a new baby in the family, and my puppy gets really worried when she cries. How can I help him stay calm?

The best thing to do is to give him lots of rewards for being near the baby, without him getting too close, or becoming anxious. If your puppy shows signs of worry, encourage him to settle elsewhere, perhaps by giving him a tasty chew to keep him occupied. Don't leave your puppy alone with the baby, as even the friendliest dog can sometimes cause problems, however unintentional that is. Once his fear begins to subside, you might find he becomes excited instead, and show attention-seeking behaviour. Again, you need to teach him to stay calm, either staying in his bed, or being near the action (but on lead). Remember that it's hard for a puppy who's been used to lots of fuss to suddenly find people's attention is now on a baby. So, make sure he's still getting lots of walks, play, training and cuddles!

Toilet-training accidents

My puppy still hasn't got the hang of going to the toilet outside. I keep finding puddles in the house, and I caught him pooing on the carpet yesterday. What can I do to improve things?

Puppies have to be taught that toileting outside is the best choice to make. The way to achieve this is to ensure that all wees and poos out of the house are rewarded with verbal praise, and a tasty food treat. If you are consistent, you will be able to put this behaviour on cue, meaning you can take your puppy into the garden and say 'hurry up!' or 'go wee wee' and he will perform. In order to reward him for going in the right place, you have to be present with him the moment he goes. You need to reward him *straight* after, for the right behaviour to be reinforced. This means managing your day so you can take your puppy into the garden regularly, perhaps every 30 minutes or so when he's awake. You need as many opportunities as possible to reward him for doing the right thing. If you know he needs to go, but hasn't, keep a very close eye on him when he comes back in the house. Keep him on a lead if necessary. Get him out again as soon as he's looking distracted and sniffing the floor, as these are signs that he's thinking about weeing or pooing.

Although it's tempting to tell a dog off for toileting indoors, it can make matters worse by creating a situation where they choose to toilet in secret (giving you even less chance to reward them for going outside in front of you). If you notice he's just about to go, you can interrupt him, and take him into the garden. But once he's started, or once he's finished (and especially after he's done ten other things before you've found the evidence), it's too late. Punishment in these moments will be ineffective and won't be linked to what you want it to be linked to. All it will do is sour your relationship with your puppy. Just clear up any mess, and plan to get him out more regularly. Persistence really does pay off, and it shouldn't be long before he realises what the rule is.

Weeing in shops

I thought it would be fun to take my puppy into the pet shop, but he did a wee on one of the displays. I was so embarrassed. Then I took him to my friend's house, and he lifted his leg on her sofa. Can I stop him from doing it again?

There are a couple of triggers that could have caused this. Aside from him just needing a wee and there being no grass nearby, he probably smelt that another dog had been there and wanted to add to that message. Or it could have been a perfectly clean site, but was at a prominent spot, and therefore a great place for him to announce that he is King of the Pet Shop. Marking behaviour increases as puppies become adolescents and young adults. You need to teach him that weeing on things outside is (usually) okay, but that he must resist when inside. Use treats to practise heelwork, sitting and staying when in the pet shop – keep his mind on other things. If he sniffs something, be ready to interrupt him if you think he's about to cock his leg and have a wee. You can say a stern 'no', then reward him for listening to you and not weeing. The more you take him into shops, the more likely he is to walk around without marking. But it's a good idea to find a 'pee post' outside but near to the shop to allow him to relieve himself *before* he enters the store, and to take him there again after your visit. Marking behaviour is stronger in some dogs, so it's a good idea to give him an outlet for this. A similar principle would apply in your friend's house – keep him on lead and close to you. Practise walking round, and reward him for lying in a bed you take with you. Don't leave him unsupervised. Take him out regularly to relieve himself in her garden, or on a short walk nearby if your friend would prefer this. Castration can sometimes reduce a male dog's need to mark their territory, but once it's become a habit you will still need to do some retraining, so it's best to start now.

Summary

Sometimes training your puppy or young dog can seem a huge chore, and you might feel you take two steps forward and one back. But keep at it. You will be rewarded by having a well-behaved adult dog, who will be a wonderful companion for years to come. Remember that prevention is better (and much quicker) than cure. Also, puppies aren't young for long, and are a wonderful source of entertainment and happiness. Celebrate your moments with them!

Good luck, and happy training!

Feedback

If you've enjoyed reading this book, and have learnt a few things that will help you with your puppy, it would be great if you felt able to leave a review on Amazon. Apart from helping other puppy owners find this book, the feedback is greatly appreciated.

You can also contact me via:

www.sarahcrockford.com

www.facebook.com/HelpingPetMinds

Thank you!

Trixie

The photos in this book are of a wonderful puppy called Trixie.

This is what her owner has to say about her:

"Trixie is a Pekalier, a cross of Pekingese and Cavalier King Charles Spaniel. She is clever yet stubborn and knows her own mind, making training an interesting but rewarding challenge. She was a shy puppy but has blossomed and is now much more outgoing, and keen to meet and charm new people. One of her favourite pastimes is chasing plant pots around the garden, sometimes with the plant still contained! Trixie's enthusiasm for life makes her such a joy to be around, she makes us smile every day, we cannot imagine life without her now."

Acknowledgements

Thanks to Mum and Dad, for always being supportive.

Thanks to Bea, for being my friend and teacher.

Thanks to all the owners I've worked with over the years, for allowing me to help you and your cheeky pups.

And thank you, whoever you are, for reading this book! I hope it has been helpful. I also hope that you have lots of fun with your puppy, both now and once they're all grown up.

Books by this author

Help! My Dog has Issues

If you've ever wondered how to improve your dog's behaviour, often the best place to start is learning to understand your dog. What are their drives, why do they do what they do?

But dogs are only half of the dog-human relationship, and as we influence them every day of their lives, you'll learn to understand a little of your own behaviour too. 'Help! My Dog Has Issues' is a common-sense guide to canine and human psychology; and sets you on a path of discovery to find behaviour and training solutions that will work for both of you.

Our Emotional Dogs

We live with dogs, and play with them, and train them - but how much do we really understand them? What are they really thinking and feeling? This book is an exploration of dog emotions, and our emotions, and what that means for the care and training of our canine friends. As well as asking 'What are emotions?', this book also shows that our dogs are sentient, conscious beings. Parts two and three of Our Emotional Dogs include personal reflections from dog owners and dog professionals.

Run or Love

Run or Love is a romantic comedy about life, love, and 'positive thinking' disasters. Suzanna has spent her life trying really hard to be perfect, and to stay in control of her life. But as her marriage falls apart, she meets her match in Freddie, who is looking for help to overcome PTSD and depression. As they both struggle to learn what they truly want from life, romance begins to blossom, but it was never going to be easy.

How to Create a Love Triangle

How to Create a Love Triangle is a romantic-comedy novella. Mel has never settled on a job or a man, but she has big dreams. When she starts her new role as a postie, and has a challenging conversation with the local film star Caroline Scarlett-Hughes, Mel starts writing to one of her fans. Not knowing she's just a postal worker, Adam writes back, imagining meeting up with Caroline and her amazing assistant. When Mel and Adam finally meet, it's going to be awkward. Meanwhile, Mel has become very good friends with a fellow worker, Ed, adding an extra complication in her search for love.

Writing Therapy

Writing Therapy focuses on two things: the therapeutic benefits of journal writing; and the enjoyment of being creative. This book will guide you through different types of personal writing, as well as poetry and short stories, and even how to start writing novels and scripts. Each chapter has five writing exercises to complete.

About the author

Sarah is a writer and pet behaviourist, who lives in Kent, England. Her assistant is black Labrador Retriever, Bea, who is always by her side. Sarah started working with animals over twenty years ago, and has been running her dog training and behaviour business since 2011. Over that time, she's met a fantastic mix of puppies and dogs, with all sorts of issues, and has loved getting to know every one of them.

Apart from working as a dog trainer and behaviourist, Sarah has a degree in equine management. She believes that animals have a lot to teach us, if only we take the time to listen and learn; and they often feature in her writing.

Sarah also runs classes and workshops for writing therapy, and creative writing.

More details can be found on her website:

www.sarahcrockford.com

Printed in Great Britain
by Amazon

28737689R00071